MW01120250

CURRENT THOUGHTS

A Study of Electricity and Magnetism

Developed by
The Agency for Instructional Technology

JOIN US ON THE INTERNET

WWW: http://www.thomson.com

EMAIL: findit@kiosk.thomson.com

A service of I(T)P®

South-Western Educational Publishing

an International Thomson Publishing company I(T)P®

Cincinnati • Albany, NY • Belmont, CA • Bonn • Boston • Detroit • Johannesburg • London • Madrid
Melbourne • Mexico City • New York • Paris • Singapore • Tokyo • Toronto • Washington

ISBN: 0-538-66857-1

2   3   4   5   6   7   8   PR   02   01   00   99   98

Printed in the United States of America

International Thomson Publishing

South-Western Educational Publishing is a division of
International Thomson Publishing, Inc.

The ITP trademark is used under license.

This book is printed on recycled, acid-free paper that meets
Environmental Protection Agency standards.

PROJECT DESIGN

Chief Consultant
Marvin Druger, Ph.D.
Department of Science Teaching
and Department of Biology
Syracuse University

Instructional Designer
Diana W. Lee, Ph.D.
Agency for Instructional Technology

Project Developer
Jonathan Greenberg, Ph.D.
Agency for Instructional Technology

PROJECT MANAGEMENT

AGENCY FOR INSTRUCTIONAL TECHNOLOGY

Director of Projects and New Products
Frank J. Batavick

Project Management Specialist
Diane Sumner

Formative Evaluation
Rockman et al.

Administrative Assistant
Connie Williamson

SOUTH-WESTERN

Vice President
Peter McBride

Publisher
Thomas A. Emrick

Project Manager
Karen Roberts

Editor
Marianne Miller

Marketing Assistant
Kris M. White

SCIENCE LINKS REVIEWERS

Gary Abbas, West High School, Davenport, Iowa; **Robert Allen**, Victor Valley Community College, Victorville, California; **Carol Bedford**, Smart Intermediate School, Davenport, Iowa; **Jennifer Braught**, Shakamak High School, Jasonville, Indiana; **Matt Braught**, Linton-Stockton High School, Linton, Indiana; **Glenda Burrus**, Pinetown High School, Pinetown, North Carolina; **Laine Gurley-Dilger**, Rolling Meadows High School, Rolling Meadows, Illinois; **Ron Endris**, Floyd Central High School, Floyds Knobs, Indiana; **Sheila Engel**, Smart Intermediate School, Davenport, Iowa; **Tom Ervin**, North High School, Davenport, Iowa; **Marcy Gaston**, Pike High School, Indianapolis, Indiana; **George Hague**, St. Mark's School of Texas, Dallas, Texas; **Mary Halsall**, Hughes Center, Cincinnati, Ohio; **Craig Leonard**, Abraham Lincoln High School, San Francisco, California; **Ann Lumsden**, Florida State University, Tallahassee, Florida; **Jim Oberdorf**, Lincoln High School, San Francisco, California; **Jan Pierson**, Bloomington North High School, Bloomington, Indiana; **Eva M. Rambo**, Bloomington South High School, Bloomington, Indiana; **Willa Ramsay**, Madison High School, San Diego, California; **Kathleen Schuehler**, Liverpool High School, Liverpool, New York; **Len Sharp**, Liverpool High School, Liverpool, New York; **Dwight Sieggreen**, Cooke Middle School, Northville, Michigan; **Gerald Skoog**, Texas Tech University, Lubbock, Texas; **Ernestine B. Smith**, Tarboro High School, Tarboro, North Carolina; **Charlotte St. Romain**, Carenco High School, Lafayette, Louisiana; **Denise Tompkins**, Southwest Edgecomb High School, Pine Tops, North Carolina; **Kevin Tsui**, Woodside High School, Woodside, California; **Rick Wells**, Central High School, Davenport, Iowa; **Eric Worch**, Indiana University, Bloomington, Indiana

---

VIDEO AND PRINT DEVELOPMENT

VIDEO

Executive Producer
David Gudaitis, Ph.D.

Associate Producer
Brad Bloom

Scriptwriter
Bob Risher

Video Editors
Amy Crowell
John MacGibbon

PRINT

Senior Editor
John Pesta

Safety Editor
Doug Mandt

Science Writers
Mary Colvard
Robert Fariel
Jonathan Greenberg, Ph.D.
Judy E. Hammett
Natasha X. Jacobs
Douglas K. Mandt
Ronald H. Morse
Michael Svec, Ph.D.

Assessment Writers
Jennifer L. Chidsey
Laura Henriques
Margaret A. Jorgensen, Ph.D.
James A. Shymansky, Ph.D.

Layout Designer/Compositor
David Strange

Cover and Page Designer
Brenda Grannan

Print and Art Coordinator
Jay Hagenow

CONTENTS

Science Links ...
Where You and Your Future Connect

You can't see them, but there are thousands of doorways in front of you ... doors to your left, doors to your right ... big doors, little doors, revolving doors, trapdoors...doors stretching into the distance as far as you can see.... Each of these doorways is a possibility, an opportunity for a successful and prosperous life. But most of the doors are locked. You need the right keys to open them. How many doors will you be able to open?

The more you learn in school, the more keys you will have ... the more choices ... the more control over your own life.

Science Links is one key to your future. In the world of tomorrow—the world of computers, robotics, the World Wide Web, gene therapy, space travel—your knowledge of science can help you keep up with the latest developments in technology. More important, it can help you find a good job and pursue a great career.

Many students consider science a difficult subject, but as you will see in this course, science can be fascinating. In *Science Links* you will learn science by doing many laboratory investigations. (Investigations that are too dangerous for the classroom will be demonstrated in video segments.) These experiments will help you understand scientific principles.

YOUR LINK TO SCIENCE

Science is an attempt to make logical sense out of the natural world. It generally involves observations, experiments, data collection, analyses, and logical conclusions. *Science Links* will let you experience science, and the experience will be informative, interesting, and fun. You will be doing many laboratory investigations that will demonstrate the importance of science in your life, both now and in your future career. Following one or more investigations, a brief reading will explain the scientific principles further.

This course gives you a great opportunity to learn about science, but the learning is up to you. Learning science can be challenging, but if you work at it, you can master the contents and processes of this fascinating field. Put your full effort into this course and you will gain the satisfaction of learning many useful things about science. More important, you will advance to the next level of your education with greater confidence, a better self-image, and a strong motivation to learn even more.

So work hard, and enjoy your *Science Links* experiences.

—Professor Marvin Druger, Past President
National Science Teachers Association

Professor Druger teaches biology at Syracuse University, where he is also chairperson of the Department of Science Teaching.

You will perform most of your investigations as a member of a small group. After your group completes its work, you and your teammates will have an opportunity to present your findings to the other students in your class. In the real world—the world of work—many jobs are based on teamwork, men and women working together to solve problems and share information.

In a few years you will be joining the adult workforce. *Science Links* can help prepare you for that important step in your life.

To give you a broad introduction to science, *Science Links* blends biology, chemistry, physics, and earth/space science into a single course. You will learn how various scientific concepts are used in the everyday world, both at home and in the workplace.

This book and the related video segments will also show you how science is used in dozens of careers, from food science to auto mechanics, from welding to respiratory therapy. Check out these careers. Maybe one of them is right for you.

When you picked up this book, you picked up a golden key. Use it now. Open the *Science Links* door, and step right in to the amazing world of science.

★ Log It!

As you perform the investigations in *Science Links*, you will record various kinds of information in a logbook. Use your logbook to take notes, to collect data, and to enter your observations and conclusions about the experiments you perform. The logbook is also a great place to jot down any questions and ideas that occur to you, either inside or outside the classroom. Put them on paper before you forget them!

If you get in the habit of using your logbook, it will help you learn to express your thoughts simply and clearly—that's good writing. The logbook will also give you a permanent record of your work—that's good science.

For more suggestions on using your logbook, see Appendix A (pages 80–81). The appendix also contains a sample logbook page.

Safety Symbols

Take appropriate precautions whenever these safety symbols appear at the beginning of the Step-by-Step instructions. All safety icons that apply to a particular investigation appear at the beginning of that investigation. In addition, a step number that is printed in **red** indicates the first time a certain kind of safety hazard exists in an investigation.

Disposal Hazard

- Dispose of this chemical only as directed.

Fire Hazard

- Tie back hair and loose clothing.
- Do not use a burner or flame near flammable materials.

Eye Hazard

- Always wear safety goggles.

Poison Hazard

- Do not chew gum, drink, or eat in the lab.
- Keep your hands and all chemicals away from your face.

Inhalation Hazard

- Avoid inhaling the substance.

Thermal-Burn Hazard

- Wear gloves and do not touch hot equipment.

Breakage Hazard

- Do not use chipped or cracked glassware.
- Do not heat the bottom of a test tube.

Corrosive-Substance Hazard

- Wear safety goggles and a lab apron.
- Do not touch any chemical.

In Case of Emergency . . .

Immediately report any accident, injury, or spill to your teacher. Know where to find the nearest fire blanket, fire extinguisher, eye-wash, sink, and shower.

Here's what to do:

Fire—Turn off all gas outlets and unplug all appliances. Use a fire blanket or fire extinguisher to smother the flames. When using a fire blanket or extinguisher to smother flames, take care not to cut off or impede the victim's air supply.

Burn—Flush the affected part with cold water.

Poisoning—Take note of the substance involved and call the teacher immediately.

Eye Injury—Flush eyes with running water; remove contact lenses. Do not allow injured persons to rub their eyes if a foreign substance is present.

Fainting—Open a window or provide fresh air as best you can. Position the person so the head is lower than the rest of the body. If breathing stops, use artificial respiration.

Spill on Skin—Flush with water.

Minor Cut—Allow to bleed briefly and then wash with soap and water. If necessary, apply a bandage.

Remember to call your teacher right away in any emergency!

module 4

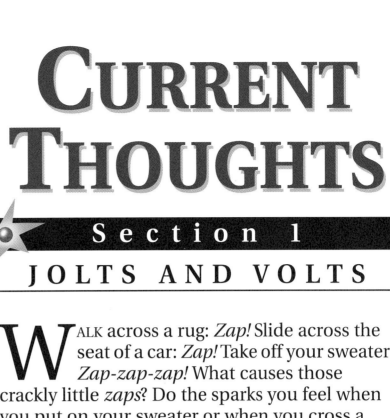

CURRENT THOUGHTS

Section 1

JOLTS AND VOLTS

WALK across a rug: *Zap!* Slide across the seat of a car: *Zap!* Take off your sweater: *Zap-zap-zap!* What causes those crackly little *zaps*? Do the sparks you feel when you put on your sweater or when you cross a carpet and open a door have anything to do with lightning? How can you prevent those shocks? How can you stop "static cling"?

There is a lot more to electricity than getting shocked. People use electricity every day of their lives, but not many of them could tell you what it is. Is it a special fluid that can travel through wires or the air? Is it some form of energy? You will explore these questions in Section 1.

What is electricity?

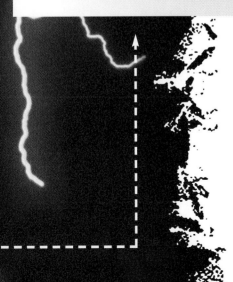

How can people "make" electricity? Where does it come from? Electric batteries have two sides, positive and negative. Magnets have north and south poles. Is there any connection between electricity and magnetism? And does electricity have anything to do with how your body works? In Sections 2–4 you will perform investigations that will help you discover the answers to these questions.

Based on what you saw in the video segment, discuss the following on-screen questions with the other members of your class.

1 How could you avoid getting shocked when you step out of a car and close the door?

2 What makes lightning jump from one cloud to another?

INVESTIGATION 1

What Is Static Electricity?

EVER WONDER?

Lightning. It's probably the biggest *zap!* you'll ever see. Did you ever watch lightning during a thunderstorm and wonder what causes the lightning and thunder? Did you notice that not all lightning bolts occur between the sky and the ground? Did you wonder why you saw the lightning flash before you heard the thunder?

Why does lightning usually occur with rain? How can you keep lightning from striking you? Why does it affect TV and radio reception? What does lightning have in common with little sparks of static electricity?

This investigation will help you learn the answers to these and other questions about electricity.

MATERIALS LIST

- 2 balloons
- 2 pieces of string (20 cm long)
- Piece of wool
- Salt
- Clear tape
- Metal pie pan
- 2 large rubber bands

STEP-BY-STEP (PART 1)

1. Blow up two balloons. Tie a 20-cm string to each one so that 15 cm of string are left to hold.

2. Rub one of the inflated balloons against a piece of wool at least 12 times, and place the balloon on the wall. Record your observations in your logbook.

3. Rub both balloons as you did in Step 2. Hold them by their strings and move them close to each other. Record your observations.

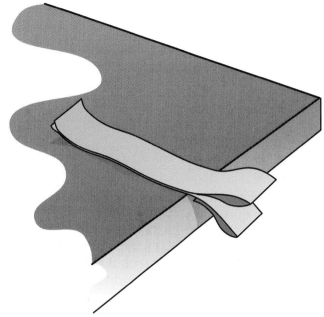

4. Rub one of the balloons as you did in Step 2, and bring it close to a small amount of salt. Record your observations.

5. Obtain a 15-cm piece of clear tape. Fold over about 1 cm of the tape at one end to serve as a nonsticky "handle."

6. Stick the tape onto a clean table so that only the handle hangs over the edge of the table (see Figure 1).

Figure 1: Equipment setup for Investigation 1, Part 1

7. Obtain another 15-cm piece of clear tape, and make a nonsticky handle as in Step 5. Neatly and firmly place this strip on top of the other strip, with the handle near the edge of the table, as in Figure 1.

8. Slowly and gently lift the bottom strip (with the top strip attached) off the table.

9. Hold the two nonsticky handles at arm's length, and pull the strips apart. Then slowly move the strips toward each other. Observe the tape strips, and record your observations.

STEP-BY-STEP (PART 2)

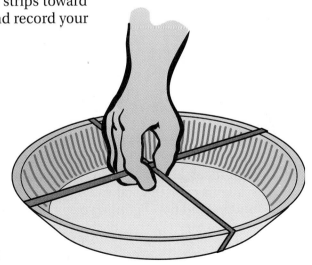

1. Place a rubber band around a clean metal pie pan. (The rubber band should cross the top and bottom of the pie pan in the middle.)

2. Do the same with a second rubber band so that it crosses the first at right angles (see Figure 2).

Figure 2: Equipment setup for Investigation 1, Part 2

3 In a semidarkened room, one member of your team should pick up the pan by holding the rubber bands where they intersect above the center of the pan. Do not touch the metal pan.

4 At the same time, the other team member should rub an inflated balloon with wool at least 12 times.

5 Without touching the pie pan, the person holding the pan should extend one finger to within 3–5 mm of the center of the pie pan, while the person holding the rubbed balloon moves it toward the bottom of the pan. Record your observations in your logbook.

6 Repeat Steps 3–5 of Part 2, but this time have the team member who is holding the pan by the rubber bands move his or her finger near the edge of the pan (instead of near the center). Record your observations.

TALK IT OVER

Work with your partner to answer the following questions.

1 What would happen if you left the charged balloon on the wall? Explain what you think would cause this to happen.

2 Which of the objects that you used had a static electric charge? How would you explain the behavior of the water and salt? What about the pie pan and balloon?

3 What causes the crackling noise when a rubbed balloon comes near the antenna of an AM radio? Do you think this effect is related to the interference caused by lightning? Explain your ideas.

4 When you see a spark or lightning, what are you actually seeing?

SPREAD THE WORD

Prepare a brief class presentation that describes what you have discovered about the behavior of static charge. You may wish to use charts and diagrams to explain your ideas. You could also repeat some steps of your investigation so that other students can see what you did. Explain how your observations can help them understand how lightning occurs.

Tell the class why this information is important in the real world. Describe some everyday situations at home or in the workplace where knowledge of static electricity and lightning would be helpful.

Science L i n k s

READ ALL ABOUT IT!

It Was a Dark and Stormy Night

JAGGED forks of lightning stab the earth and splinter across the sky. Houses tremble in the powerful roar of thunder. . . . Lightning and thunder—they're the stuff of horror movies and mystery novels. But what is lightning? Is it nothing more than a gigantic spark of static electricity? The solution to this mystery can be found in the structure of the atom.

If you are not already familiar with atomic structure, here is a brief summary: Everything—every kind of matter—is composed of atoms. The center of an atom is called the **nucleus** (see Figure 3). One or more **protons** are inside the nucleus, and each proton has one unit of positive electric charge. Most atoms also contain one or more **neutrons** in the nucleus. Neutrons have no electric charge. Spinning around the nucleus are a number of much smaller particles called **electrons**. Each electron has one unit of negative electric charge.

Atoms usually have an equal number of protons and electrons, making them electrically neutral. However, electrons can jump from one atom or molecule to another. The atom that gains electrons becomes negatively charged, while the atom that loses electrons becomes positively charged. Because these charges tend to *stay* on an object, this process of electron switching is called **static electricity**. (The word "static" means something that does not change or move.) On the other hand, charges that move through a wire are called **current electricity**.

CLOUDS OF ELECTRONS

Getting back to lightning, how does a cloud in the sky accumulate enough charge to create a lightning bolt? In Investigation 1 you saw that rubbing certain materials together can cause them to become charged. When you rubbed a balloon against a piece of wool, electrons were transferred from one object to the other. The object that gained electrons became negatively charged, and the object that lost electrons was left with a positive charge. Up in the clouds, less solid objects

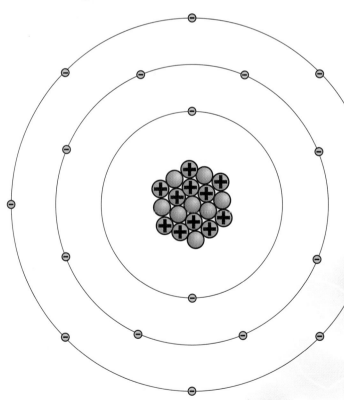

Figure 3: Structure of an atom (greatly simplified)
Note: Positively charged protons (yellow) and neutral neutrons (blue) in the nucleus are surrounded by negatively charged electrons (lavender). Normally the numbers of protons and electrons are equal.

are rubbing against one another. Air circulates within the clouds. Upward drafts carry droplets of water past falling ice crystals. As the drops of liquid water and the crystals of ice brush past one another, some electrons pass from the droplets to the crystals. The positively charged liquid droplets travel up to the tops of the clouds, and the negatively charged ice crystals accumulate near the bottoms. This is one way that cloud tops become positive and their bottoms become negative.

When you brought your finger close to the pie pan, excess electrons were able to jump through the air between your finger and the pan, creating a spark. This could not occur until the difference in charge between your finger and the pan was great enough and the distance between them was small enough. Similarly, when enough charge builds up on a cloud, a gigantic spark can carry excess electrons from a negatively charged part of the cloud to a more positively charged area. The spark can occur within a single cloud, or it can jump to a different cloud, or it can strike the ground.

If the clouds are the objects that are electrically charged, what makes lightning strike the ground? Think about your experiment with the balloon and

salt. Although you did not rub anything on the salt, it jumped. As you observed, objects with similar charges (positive or negative) repel each other, while objects with opposite charges attract each other. Charged objects can also attract neutral objects. When you brought the balloon close to the salt, the negative charge of the balloon repelled the electrons in the salt, and some of them moved away, leaving the part of the salt pile near the balloon positive. Now the positive part of the salt was attracted to the negative balloon (see Figure 4).

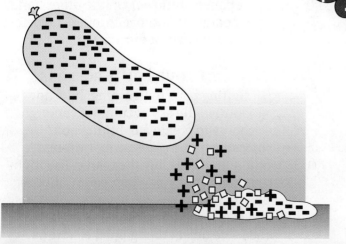

Figure 4: Effect of charged objects on neutral objects
Note: Negative charges repel electrons in neutral objects, making the facing surface positive. This can cause attraction (left) or a spark (right).

LEADING THE CHARGE

Benjamin Franklin was one of the Founding Fathers of the United States, and he was one of the first American scientists.

Born in 1706, Franklin experimented with electricity at a time when people knew almost nothing about it. The famous experiment in which he flew a kite during a thunderstorm was part of his effort to understand the connection between electricity and lightning.

Although Franklin had no formal scientific training, he was an excellent observer who carried out careful, precise experiments. Among his contributions was the discovery that two types of electric charge exist. He called the charges "positive" and "negative."

Franklin also applied his knowledge in useful ways: In the eighteenth century, lightning was a frequent cause of house fires, but the lightning rod that he invented reduced this danger, saving lives and property.

CHARGE!

Something similar happens when a highly charged cloud passes over the ground. Electrons in the highest points on the ground—trees, buildings, hilltops—are repelled by the negative cloud bottoms. These electrons flow down into the ground. As the objects on the surface become positively charged, the difference in charge between them and the clouds increases until a huge spark of lightning jumps through the air.

Lightning bolts are extremely hot and bright. They may shine as brightly as a million 100-watt bulbs and heat the air up to 28,000°C. This heating causes a sudden and violent expansion of this strip of air, which smashes against the air around it and produces the sound of thunder.

Thunderstorms can occur at any time, but they are most frequent and intense during the late spring and summer months. Usually they occur in the late afternoon or early evening because the air near the earth's surface has been heated during the day and rises. As this warm air rises, it cools. Its cooling water vapor forms trillions of tiny water droplets—clouds.

STRIKING DISTANCE

To calculate how far away a bolt of lightning is, figure that every five seconds between the time you see the lightning and hear the thunder equals a distance of one mile. Even though lightning and thunder occur at almost the same moment, you see the lightning first because light travels faster than sound. Light travels at 300,000 kilometers per second. Sound travels only about 340 meters per second. The light reaches you almost instantly, but the sound takes a little bit longer.

ON YOUR OWN

Respond to the following items based on "It Was a Dark and Stormy Night."

1 How would you explain that thunderstorms seldom occur during cold winter weather?

2 During a thunderstorm, why would you be safer sitting in a car with a metal roof than standing in a parking lot?

3 Tiny pieces of paper will first "jump" onto a charged balloon, but then many jump away. Give the reasons for this.

INVESTIGATION 2

No Static, Please

EVER WONDER?

People use electricity all the time—at home, in school, at work, on vacation, everywhere. The modern world could hardly exist without electricity. Yet most people take it for granted. In fact, they know almost nothing about it.

When you switch on the lights in your room, what happens in the electric lines that extend from your home to the power plant? How is the electricity that runs through a lightbulb and brightens your room different from the static electricity that causes lightning? In this investigation you will begin to explore electric currents and discover how they behave.

MATERIALS LIST

- 2 D-cells
- Lightbulb
- 3 pieces of wire
- Adhesive tape
- Flashlight
- Lantern battery
- Steel wool
- Balloon
- Safety goggles

ELECTRICIAN

Electricians have many job possibilities. They can work either as independent contractors or as employees of electrical firms and other companies. Working with electricity is dangerous, and so it is important to be well-trained and knowledgeable about safety procedures. To become a licensed electrician, the first thing you need is a high school diploma. The next step is to serve as an apprentice under a licensed, or journeyman, electrician. During your apprenticeship, you may be required to take technical courses. Eventually you must pass a state test based on the national electrical code. Once you are a journeyman, you can set your sights on becoming a master electrician. To reach this level, you must have complete knowledge of the trade and pass another test. For more information about careers in electricity, write:

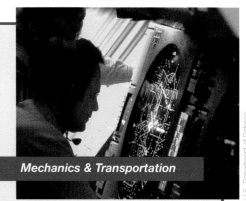

Mechanics & Transportation

U.S. Department of Defense

National Electrical Contractors Association
3 Bethesda Metro Center, Suite 1100
Bethesda, MD 20814
http://www.necanet.org

Related occupations: electrical contractor, electrical safety inspector, lighting technician, sound technician, telephone or cable-TV installer

STEP-BY-STEP

1. Using one D-cell, one bulb, and one wire, find a way to make the lightbulb glow. Draw a picture in your logbook of how you arranged the equipment.

2. Find other arrangements of the bulb, battery, and wire that will light the bulb. (Find as many as possible.) Sketch in your logbook each arrangement that lights the bulb.

3. Reverse the positive and negative ends of the D-cell. Record your observations in your logbook.

4. Place two D-cells tightly end-to-end and facing in the same direction. Tape their sides together to hold them in place. This is called a "two-cell battery."

5. Connect the two-cell battery to the bulb, making it glow. Note the intensity at which it glows. Sketch your equipment, and record your observations in your logbook.

6. Inflate the balloon, and tie the opening shut.

7. Put on your safety goggles.

8. Straighten a single strand of steel wool, and tape it to the balloon. Leave the ends of the wire free.

9 Attach the lantern battery to the strand of steel wool and to a bulb so that the bulb lights. If necessary, you may use one additional short piece of wire to join the parts together. Allow the bulb to stay lit for up to five minutes, if possible. Record your observations.

10 Open and examine the inside of a flashlight. Describe in your logbook the series of parts that connect the cells (batteries) to the bulb. Also sketch these parts.

TALK IT OVER

Work with your partner(s) to answer the following questions.

1 How must a battery be connected to a bulb in order for the bulb to glow? What does this tell you about how current electricity flows?

2 How did the electrons move when you made the bulb glow? Describe the path of the electrons through your equipment.

3 What changed when you reversed the direction of the battery in Step 3? How did this affect the glow of the bulb? Explain your ideas.

4 How did the addition of a second cell affect the brightness of the bulb? Explain what happened.

5 What might happen if you constructed a 10-cell battery and connected it to one bulb?

6 What broke the balloon? What was the source of the force or energy that broke it?

UFO OR ST. ELMO?

In the past, sailors were often puzzled by a greenish glow that hovered around the masts of their ships. They called this mysterious light "St. Elmo's fire," naming it after the patron saint of sailors.

St. Elmo's fire is not really fire. It is discharged electricity. Most objects have very little charge; however, a static charge sometimes builds up in an object as it moves through a nonconducting material. The glow of St. Elmo's fire results from the steady discharge of stored electricity in water or wind (moving air).

You don't have to be aboard a ship to see St. Elmo's fire. People on airplanes have observed it around propellers and wingtips, and people on the ground have seen it around fuel tanks and nozzles. So if *you* happen to see a flickering greenish glow in the sky, it's probably not a UFO. More likely it's St. Elmo.

SPREAD THE WORD

Work with your partner(s) to prepare a presentation. Share with the other members of the class what you have learned about how electricity flows through wires.

You could demonstrate how you carried out the investigation, and you could create neat drawings of how you attached your equipment. Be sure to explain what you learned from each activity that you performed.

Think of some practical applications for the ideas you have developed. Give several examples of how knowledge of current electricity is used in everyday life and in different kinds of work.

The Force behind the Current

Whan happens when electricity flows through a wire? Your work in Investigation 2 revealed some important clues about current electricity. When you turn on a light, motor, or other electrical device, you use a switch. Turning on the switch connects the ends of two wires. This connection completes a **circuit**, or loop. For example, the circuit may run from a wall plug through a lightbulb and back to the wall plug.

Think back to Investigation 2, where you discovered that the bulb would light only when there was a complete circuit connecting the battery and the bulb. When the circuit was complete, electrons could flow from the battery, through the wire, through the bulb, and back to the battery. The electrons continued flowing as long as the circuit was intact (unbroken).

6,240,000,000,000,000,000

It is possible to measure how much electric current flows through a wire. To understand how this is done, think of a current of electricity as a current of water. If you wanted to describe how fast a river is flowing, you could say that a certain number of liters flows past a certain point every second. (For example, the river may be flowing at a rate of 10,000 liters per second.) The size of an

electric current is measured in **amperes** ("amps"). One amp is 6.24 billion billion electrons (6,240,000,000,000,000,000) passing a certain point every second. The total electric charge on this many electrons is called a **coulomb**.

Just as water tends to flow downhill . . . electrons tend to flow down an "energy hill."

On the back or bottom of many electrical appliances, the manufacturer lists the amperage of that device. This figure shows the amount of current that passes through the appliance when it is running. A 100-watt lightbulb has approximately one amp flowing through its filament every second.

ROUND AND ROUND

What causes the current to flow? Just as water tends to flow downhill (losing gravitational potential energy as it goes), electrons tend to flow down an "energy hill." The electrons flow from a place where they have a great deal of potential energy to a place where they have less (see Figure 5).

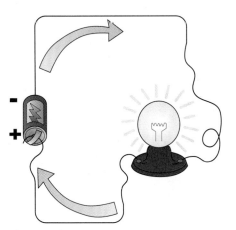
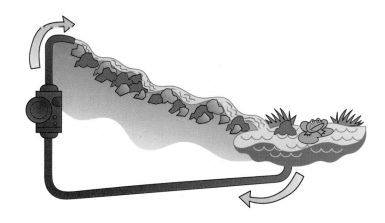

Figure 5: Complete circuits
Note: Electric current and an artificial waterfall can flow as long as the current or water can travel in a complete circle. If either loop is broken, the flow will stop.

Here's how this works in an electric cell, such as a flashlight battery: Chemical reactions inside the battery release electrons into the metal tip at one end of the cell. Because so many electrons are crowded together at that spot, they repel one another. The force they exert on one another gives them electrical potential energy, and so they can move out into the wire. However, just as water loses potential energy as it flows downhill, the electrons lose energy as they flow away from the battery.

The electron current flows through the wire and the lightbulb and returns to the other end of the cell, replacing electrons that are just leaving. If you look closely at an electric cell, you will see that its ends are labeled with plus and minus signs. Electrons are released at the negative end with lots of potential energy, and they return to the positive end, where their potential energy is much lower.

PENNY POWER

The energy that a battery gives to electrons is called **potential**, or **voltage**. Electrical potential is measured in **volts**. The D-cells used in a flashlight provide 1.5 volts each. An electrical socket in the wall provides 110–120 volts. How much energy does one volt provide? You can get some idea of this by putting 40 pennies in a small bag and dropping it. After the bag falls one meter, it will have one **joule** of energy. If you catch the bag at that point, the impact—the force of its kinetic energy—feels like the amount of energy provided by one volt.

One volt provides one joule of energy to one coulomb of electrons. That is the energy that pushes electrons through an electrical circuit. The greater the voltage, the more current will flow. During Investigation 2, when you increased the number of cells in your circuit from one to two, you doubled the voltage. This doubled the number of electrons flowing through the bulb every second. Because more energy was available to the bulb, it glowed more brightly. The electrons lost some of their energy as they did the work of making the bulb glow.

TAKE A BREAK

If voltage is too high, electrical devices can be damaged. Computers and other expensive machines are often plugged into surge protectors, which in turn are plugged into wall sockets. Surge protectors are a good idea because sometimes the voltage supplied by the wall socket "surges"—it jumps briefly to a higher-than-normal value. When this happens, too many electrons (too much current) with too much energy (too high a voltage) pass through the computer. All that extra energy can damage the equipment. Remember what happened to the balloon in Investigation 2: Too much current and voltage for the thin strand of steel wool produced a great deal of heat energy, which melted part of the balloon, causing it to explode.

Besides using devices that protect against surges, you can use **fuses** to safeguard electrical equipment.

A wire inside the fuse melts when the current and voltage get too high. This melting wire breaks the circuit, protecting the expensive equipment. The fuse must then be replaced.

A more convenient means of protection is a **circuit breaker**, which is simply an automatic switch that turns the circuit off during a voltage surge. You do not need to replace the circuit breaker every time it goes off—you just switch it back on.

Fuses and circuit breakers are also safety devices: If too many electrical items are running on the same circuit, the wiring might get too hot, causing a fire. A fuse that blows out while you are watching TV and making popcorn and drying your hair and playing the stereo and doing on-line research might just save your life.

Surge protectors are designed to prevent damage to computers and other devices when the voltage supplied by a wall socket "surges"—jumps briefly to a higher-than-normal value.

ON YOUR OWN

Answer the following questions based on "The Force behind the Current."

1 What happens to the energy that electrons lose as they pass through a lightbulb?

2 Where do electrons go after passing through a lightbulb? Do they accumulate somewhere? Are they sent out through the glass bulb with the light? Do they return to the battery or generator where they started? Explain your ideas.

3 When electrons pass through the heating wires in a toaster and return to the power source, do they still have as much energy as they did when they started? Describe the sequence of energy transfers in a toaster.

INVESTIGATION 3

Not All Circuits Are Alike

EVER WONDER?

Have you ever been outside at sunset and noticed that the streetlights came on all at once? Did you wonder how the lights are hooked up? Are they connected in a single line, with the same current flowing through all of them? If so, why don't they all go dark when one bulb burns out? How big can a circuit be? Is there a limit to how many lights can be lit by the same power source? This investigation will help you discover the answers to these questions as you learn about different kinds of circuits.

MATERIALS LIST

- Drinking straws
- Beverage stirrers (hollow)
- Scissors
- Paper cups
- 2 D-cells
- Tape
- 3 pieces of insulated wire with bare ends
- 3 lightbulbs with sockets
- 2 paper clips
- Refills for mechanical pencils (thick and thin pieces of graphite)

STEP-BY-STEP (PART 1)

1 If your teacher asks you to carry out this part of the investigation, start by filling a paper cup with water.

2 Squeeze one end of a drinking straw just enough to allow it to be inserted into the end of another straw. Connect the two straws so that you have one long straw.

3 Cut a short piece off a third straw. Make this piece of straw just long enough to let you drink through it.

4 Try drinking the water in your cup. First use the short piece of straw; then use the extra-long straw. Record in your logbook how easy or difficult it is to drink through each straw.

5 Cut a piece of straw the same length as a beverage stirrer. Try drinking through each of these items. Record your observations.

TALK IT OVER (PART 1)

Because you worked alone in Part 1, answer the following questions in your logbook. When you finish writing down your answers, discuss them with the rest of the class.

1 Is it easier for water to flow through a long tube or a short one?

2 Is it easier for water to flow through a wide tube or a narrow one?

3 How can these results help you predict how easily electric current flows through long narrow objects and short wide ones? Explain your ideas, and record your prediction.

STEP-BY-STEP (PART 2)

1 Assemble the equipment as in Figure 6.

2 Touch the two paper clips together. Observe the brightness of the bulb.

3 Lay a thin refill for a mechanical pencil on the table. Touch both paper clips to the refill close together at one end. Observe the brightness of the bulb.

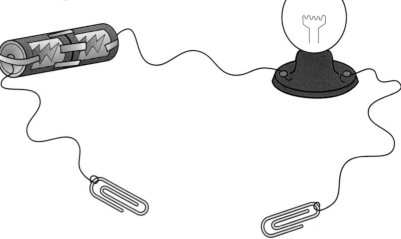

Figure 6: Equipment setup for the first five steps of Investigation 3, Part 2

4 Continue holding the clips against the refill. Slowly move one of the clips along the length of the refill so that a longer and longer section of the refill connects the two paper clips. Observe the brightness of the bulb as you do this. Record in your logbook the observations you have made in Steps 3 and 4.

5 Repeat Steps 3 and 4, but this time use a thick refill.

6 Remove the paper clips from the circuit. Attach the free ends of the wires to a second lightbulb (see Figure 7).

Figure 7: Equipment setup for Steps 6 and 7

7 Observe the brightness of the bulbs. Record your observations in your logbook.

8 Insert a third bulb in the circuit between the first two bulbs.

9 Observe the brightness of the bulbs, and record your observations.

Current Thoughts

10 Remove two of the bulbs from the circuit, and join the free ends of the wires so that the bulb lights.

11 Attach a second bulb to the circuit alongside the first (see Figure 8).

12 Observe the brightness of the bulbs. Record your observations in your logbook.

13 Attach a third bulb alongside the first two. Observe the brightness of the bulbs, and record your observations.

14 Return all materials according to your teacher's instructions.

Figure 8: Equipment setup for Steps 11 and 12

Talk It Over (Part 2)

Work with the other members of your group to answer these questions:

1 When the bulb stopped glowing in Step 4, did the current stop flowing? Explain.

2 Did the current travel throughout the entire refill or only through the portion between the paper clips?

3 How did the length of the refill between the paper clips affect the brightness of the bulb?

4 When is it easier to light more than one bulb with the same power source—when the bulbs are all connected in a series (Steps 6–9) or when each bulb is connected directly to the battery (Steps 11–13)?

5 Did all the current go through all the bulbs when they were connected in a series (Steps 6–9)? Did all the current go through all the bulbs when each bulb was connected directly to the battery (Steps 11–13)?

6 In which type of circuit do you think the current lost the most energy while passing through the bulbs? Explain your ideas.

7 What would happen if you connected 100 bulbs in series to a two-cell battery?

8 What would happen if you connected 100 bulbs directly to a two-cell battery?

9 How are your observations of the two kinds of circuits that you built in Part 2 of this investigation similar to the observations that you made in Part 1?

10 If you were a city planner, how would you connect the streetlights—in series, or directly to the power supply? Explain your decision.

SPREAD THE WORD

To help other students understand what you have learned in this investigation, present your results to the class. Explain what you have discovered about how current travels through the two kinds of circuits you built. Tell how the thickness and length of an object affect the currents that travel through it. Also explain how these two ideas are related. Include in your presentation neat drawings of the circuits you made.

List some examples of each of the two kinds of circuits that you built. Try to come up with situations at home and the workplace. Tell who would benefit from knowing how circuits and other objects affect the flow of electric currents.

READ ALL ABOUT IT!

Voltage, Current, Resistance, Power

THINK about water flowing through a pipe in the walls of your home. The longer and narrower the pipe, the more slowly the water flows through it. The tight pathway in the pipe resists the flow of water. Similarly, an electrical circuit resists the flow of electric current. That is why a voltage is needed to make the current flow.

As you learned in Investigation 3, a long narrow part of a circuit increases the resistance of the circuit more than a short wide part does. (It's the same with water: Water flows more easily through the plumbing if you replace narrow pipes with wider ones or if you shorten the distance that the water must travel.)

An electrical device, such as a lightbulb or a motor, has a certain amount of resistance. If you wire several items in a series, you increase the resistance of the circuit. That cuts down the current; therefore, less energy is available to run the motors or light the bulbs. This kind of circuit is known as a **series circuit** (see Figure 7 on page 15). The bulbs or motors are said to be connected "in series."

CONNECTED IN PARALLEL

If you connect bulbs alongside one another so that each one is connected directly to a battery or some other power source, each one will experience the same voltage. They will all light up (unless there are so many that they drain all the energy out of the battery). This type of circuit is called a **parallel circuit** (see Figure 8). The electrical devices are said to be connected "in parallel."

Go back to those water pipes again. If you connected several pipes in parallel, water would

HOW DO LIGHTNING BUGS LIGHT UP?

A lightning bug (firefly) is a tiny beetle that uses light organs on its abdomen to produce the yellowish glimmering glow you see on summer nights. Its light organs are little chemical generators that mix the chemical luciferin and the enzyme luciferase with oxygen to produce a form of light.

Lightning bugs use energy far more efficiently than people do. When a lightning bug lights up, only five percent of its chemical energy is lost as heat. In contrast, when an ordinary lightbulb is switched on, 90 percent of the electrical energy that the bulb uses is wasted as heat—only 10 percent of the energy produces light!

be able to flow more easily because it could use more pathways. Similarly, when you connect lightbulbs in parallel, you provide more pathways for the electric current that passes through the circuit. On the other hand, if you connect lightbulbs in series, you lengthen the circuit, and this increases the resistance. In a long series you may not have enough current to light all the bulbs.

OHM'S LAW

Another way you could increase the flow of water through a long and narrow pipe would be to add a powerful pump. The same is true of electricity: You can overcome the resistance of the circuit and increase the flow of current by increasing the voltage. Current, voltage, and resistance are all related to one another. The higher the voltage, the more current results. But the greater the resistance, the less current can flow. These relationships are described by **Ohm's Law**, which says that current *(I)* is equal to voltage *(V)* divided by resistance *(R)*. Resistance is measured in units called **ohms**.

$$I = \frac{V}{R}$$

WHAT'S A WATT?

What makes a 100-watt lightbulb brighter than a 60-watt bulb? And what is a watt? A 100-watt bulb converts more electrical energy (voltage) to light than a smaller bulb does. You could say it is more powerful. The **power** of a bulb (and any other device) is the rate at which it converts energy from one form, such as electrical voltage, to another, such as light. Power is measured in **watts**. One watt is equal to one joule of energy per second.

All electrical devices convert electrical energy to other forms. Their power depends

GET THIS . . .

Ohm's Law

To determine how much current will flow through a wire, divide the voltage by the resistance.

$$I \text{ (current)} = \frac{V}{R}$$

CAREER LINKS

Communication Technologies

BROADCAST TECHNICIAN

If you're like most people, you get most of your news and entertainment from TV and radio. These devices convert electronic signals to pictures or sounds. The job of a broadcast technician is to set up, monitor, and adjust the equipment that is used to transmit video and audio signals. You can get hands-on experience in this field early by building your own ham radio or by assembling hobby kits. High school courses in math, physics, industrial arts, and household arts provide an excellent background. Some technicians obtain additional training or certification from a technical school or community college. For more information about career opportunities, write:

Society of Broadcast Engineers
8445 Keystone Crossing, Suite 140
Indianapolis, IN 46240
http://www.sbe.org

Related occupations: technical operator, science technician, medical-laboratory technician, electronics engineer

on both the current and the voltage that they receive. The greater the current and voltage, the more work an appliance can do. Power increases as either the voltage or the current increases. Power *(P)* is equal to current *(I)* multiplied by voltage *(V)*:

$$P = IV$$

POWER PLAY

If you want to know how much energy your refrigerator, computer, or television is using, just multiply the power by the length of time you use it. For example, suppose you have a lamp that uses a 60-watt bulb and you left it burning for five hours. One hour is equal to 3,600 seconds; therefore, five hours are equal to 18,000 seconds.

$$
\begin{array}{r}
18{,}000 \ \text{seconds} \\
\times \ 60 \ \text{watts} \\
\hline
= \ 1{,}080{,}000 \ \text{joules}
\end{array}
$$

That's a lot of energy. Electric companies usually list the cost of electric power on the

monthly bill in units of kilowatt-hours; one kilowatt-hour is the amount of energy used by a 1,000-watt device in one hour, or 3,600,000 joules. With this information, you can figure out what it costs to run any electrical device in your home.

ON YOUR OWN

Answer the following questions based on "Voltage, Current, Resistance, Power."

1 How could you get more current to flow through a particular wire?

2 How could you construct a circuit so that it would have more resistance?

3 How would you explain that electrical appliances use more power when a large current flows through them?

SECTION WRAP-UP

Writing with Power

WHAT a day. You've been at your computer for hours, trying to finish writing a paper about electricity. Now it's starting to thunder, and you start to worry that lightning might knock out the power before you are done working. As you stare toward the window at the evening sky, you notice the sound of the computer's fan motor. It keeps humming quietly, blowing hot air out the back of the machine. You think about what causes the computer to heat up: It resists the flow of electricity through it. As electrons flow through the circuits, they lose some of their energy. The computer warms up as that energy is converted to heat. The fan's job is to blow air through the computer, keeping the circuits cooler.

SOME LIGHTS STAYED ON

The heat from the computer also warms the room a little bit—very little. The electric baseboard heater along the wall warms the room a lot more. That's because the heater has a much higher resistance than the computer. And because of the greater resistance, much less current flows through the heater than the computer, even though both of them are plugged in to the same 120-volt socket. Electrons that pass through the heater lose more energy than the ones that pass through the computer: The heater has more power than the computer. Most of that energy is converted to heat.

Lightning flickers in the distance, followed by rumbles of thunder a few seconds later because sound travels more slowly than light. Then suddenly, *zap-boom!*—there's a bright flash of lightning down the street, and this time you hear the crash of thunder sooner. It's darker outside now. You get up to look out the window. The rain is coming down hard and fast, pelting the glass like pebbles.

The dark clouds overhead have positively charged tops and negatively charged bottoms.

Two blocks away, the streetlights have gone out. What a coincidence—you just finished writing about series and parallel circuits, and you realize that the streetlights must be connected in parallel. If they had all been connected in series, every streetlight in town would be dark, but the ones on your street are still working. The parallel streetlight circuits all receive the same voltage, but the current is divided among them; therefore, only a small part of the total current passes through each lamp. In a series circuit, all the current would pass through every lamp, but only a small part of the voltage would be available to each one.

You know about lightning. The dark clouds overhead have positively charged tops and negatively charged bottoms. One of these thunderclouds must have passed over a tall object, maybe a tree. As it did, the negative charge on the cloud bottom pushed electrons down out of the tree into the ground. This gave the top of the tree a positive charge. The difference in charge between the bottom of the cloud and the top of the tree became so great that a huge spark shot through the air, carrying excess electrons from the cloud through the tree and into the ground. For a moment the voltage, which was caused by the static charges on the cloud and tree, produced a current that carried the electrons to the ground.

Hmmm, maybe it's time to turn off the computer. Lightning can do a lot of damage:

If it gets into the house's electrical system, it might fry your friendly computer, even though the machine is plugged into a surge protector, which is designed to prevent a sudden jump in voltage from damaging the circuits.

CHARGING THE TONER

As soon as the storm passes, you switch on the computer again and get back to work. All you need to finish your paper is an example of a practical use of static electricity. Then—*zappo!*—it comes to you. Quickly you finish writing and send your document to the printer. As the pages begin to slide out of the printer, you think about what you have just written: "The printer uses electrical current to collect static charge and transfer it to each part of the page where a letter will be printed, and it puts an opposite charge on the black toner powder. The toner particles stick to the charged parts of the paper, and a heater fuses them together."

You pick up the still-warm pages and put them in your folder. This paper is not just *about* electricity. You used current and static electricity to write and print it. More important, you understand how it all works.

ON YOUR OWN

Answer the following questions based on "Writing with Power."

1 Is it possible to use the static charges that lead to lightning to generate electric current? What might be some of the problems with such a plan?

2 How would you explain the fact that lamps and most other electrical appliances in your home use 120 volts but washing machines and dryers often require 220 volts? What does this tell you about the resistance of these devices and the amount of work they do?

3 Portable radios and other battery-powered devices are often powered by a set of cells connected in series. What is the advantage of connecting the cells in series rather than in parallel?

This woman is either having a very bad hair day or there is a lot of static electricity in her hair. If each strand of hair has the same kind of charge, the hairs repel one another.

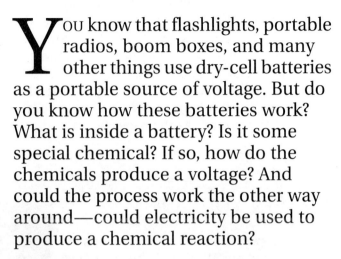

Y<small>OU</small> know that flashlights, portable radios, boom boxes, and many other things use dry-cell batteries as a portable source of voltage. But do you know how these batteries work? What is inside a battery? Is it some special chemical? If so, how do the chemicals produce a voltage? And could the process work the other way around—could electricity be used to produce a chemical reaction?

The investigations you perform in Section 2 will help you answer these questions, as you learn about the link between chemicals and electricity.

You will also learn about the link between metals and electricity. You will learn the reasons that metals carry electricity so well, and you'll explore whether some metals are better than others for carrying electric currents. How do jewelry makers use electricity to coat cheaper metals with silver or gold? How do computers use electricity to handle information? You'll discover the answers to all these questions. Start by watching the next video segment.

FREEZE FRAME

Now that you have watched the video segment, discuss the following on-screen questions with the other students in your class.

1 Is it accurate to call a battery the opposite of an electroplating apparatus? What does that mean?

2 If computers and telegraphs use the same principle of digital coding, what is the advantage of a computer?

Electricity Express

EVER WONDER?

Most electrical wires are covered with a layer of plastic. Why is that covering needed? Does electric current pass more easily through some materials than others? When you were little, your mother or father probably warned you never to use a light switch if your hands were wet. Why? Does electric current travel easily through water? In this investigation you will discover how electricity travels through various materials.

MATERIALS LIST

- Lantern battery (6 v)
- Lightbulb
- 3 insulated wires (20 cm long) with ends stripped
- 3 paper clips
- Spoon
- Salt
- Sugar
- 3 small cups (plastic or paper)
- Distilled or deionized water
- Samples for electrical testing
- Safety goggles

STEP-BY-STEP

1 Put on your safety goggles.

2 Assemble the apparatus as in Figure 9. Wrap the bare ends of the wires around the paper clips. If necessary, tape the wires in place.

3 Touch the paper clips together to be sure that the bulb lights.

4 In your logbook create a data table with three columns. Put "Sample" over the first column, "Prediction" over the second, and "Observations" over the third.

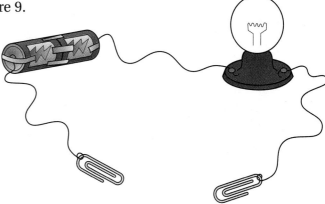

Figure 9: Equipment setup for Investigation 4

5 In the "Sample" column, list each of the materials that your teacher has provided for testing.

6 Discuss with your partner(s) which sample materials you think will carry an electric current from one of your paper clips to the other, making the bulb light. Record your prediction for each sample in the data table.

7 Test the materials by touching the two ends of each sample with the paper clips. For each sample, record the bulb's brightness in the "Observations" column.

8 Put some sugar into a plastic or paper cup.

9 Test the ability of the sugar to carry electric current. (Stick the paper clips in the sugar.) Record the results in your table.

10 Pour some distilled water into a different cup.

11 Test the water by inserting the ends of the paper clips in it. Record the results.

12 Put sugar in the water. Use a spoon to stir the sugar and water into a solution.

13 Test the sugar-water solution, and record the results in your table.

14 Thoroughly rinse the cups and spoon with tap water; then rinse them with a little bit of distilled water. Dry them with clean paper towels.

15 Repeat Steps 8–13 using salt instead of sugar.

16 Clean up your work area. Return materials as your teacher directs.

POLAR LIGHT SHOWS

If you lived at the north or south pole, you would see fantastic light shows all year round. You would see colorful arcs brightening and flickering as they streak through the sky. Sometimes these brilliant displays stretch 1,000 kilometers across the sky and are visible over much of the earth.

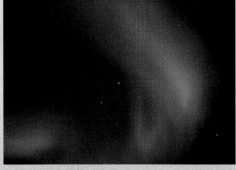

The fireworks at the north pole are called the northern lights or the "aurora borealis," a name that comes from Aurora, the Roman goddess of dawn.

The flashes of light are caused by electrically charged particles that the sun emits. Traveling through space, these particles form what is known as the solar wind. Earth's magnetic field traps some of the particles, which then collide with other atoms and molecules in the atmosphere, releasing energy and lighting up the skies.

The south pole also has a strong magnetic field that attracts and traps the solar wind. Here the energy release is called the southern lights or the "aurora australis." In both places, the intensity of the light shows depends on the number of particles that the sun emits. The more particles that the sun discharges, the more particles the earth will trap.

About every 11 years the sun becomes highly active electrically. If you can see an aurora during one of the sun's active periods, you will see an especially good show, with brighter and more flaring colors.

SCIENCE TECHNICIAN

A science technician operates and maintains the equipment that scientists use to carry out their experiments and to collect data. In other words, they run the electronic tools of the scientists. A tech might set up remote sensors in the field, help design a new computer model in the lab, and do many other challenging jobs. To become a science technician, you will need at least an associate's degree from a junior or community college. Get as much hands-on experience with lab or computer equipment as you can. This kind of practical experience will give you a real edge when you go looking for a job. For more information, use a directory to find a society that represents the science in which you are interested. If that science happens to be chemistry, write:

Engineering Technologies

American Chemical Society
Education Division
1155 16th Street, N.W.
Washington, DC 20036
http://www.acs.org

Related occupations: health technologist, agricultural and biological technicians, medical technologist, computer-systems analyst

TALK IT OVER

Work with your partner(s) to answer the following questions.

1   Based on your observations, what kinds of materials seem to carry electricity well?

2   What might be a reason that electric current passes more easily through some materials than others?

3   The human body is made up mostly of water. Would you expect a person's body to carry electric current well?

4   What would be a reason to avoid turning lights on or off with wet hands? What if you had pickle juice or pancake syrup on your hands—which would be more dangerous? Explain your ideas.

SPREAD THE WORD

RESULTS

Work with your partner or the other members of your group to prepare a presentation. Tell the class what you have learned about various kinds of materials and how well they can carry electric currents. If you want to give a dramatic presentation, you could write and perform a skit demonstrating safe and unsafe behavior around electrical equipment or downed power lines. You could also demonstrate how you used your materials, and you could display your results on a poster or an overhead transparency.

Describe some possible jobs or other situations in which your conclusions would be useful. (You could include this information in the dramatic skit by having some characters encounter electrical hazards at their homes or in their jobs.) Be sure to explain how to avoid getting an electrical shock.

Read All about It!

Electrical Conductivity (and Safe Conduct)

WHEN you carried out Investigation 4, it was probably no surprise that electric current passed easily through metals but not so well through most other solids. The ability of a material to carry an electric current is called its **conductivity**. Metals are good conductors.

Materials that do not conduct current well are called **insulators**. Plastic is a good insulator. That is why it is used in electrical wires: It keeps current in the wire, and it keeps current out of any nearby metal parts that the wire might touch. Glass and ceramics are other good insulators. (You may have noticed glass and ceramic insulators on poles with electric power lines.)

Why are metals so good at conducting electricity? The answer has to do with the structure of their atoms. The electrons in an atom are arranged at various distances from the nucleus, somewhat like planets orbiting the sun. In metals, the electrons in the outermost orbits are held only loosely to the atom. These loose outer electrons can wander from one atom to the next. Instead of being part of individual atoms, they form

Plastic is a good insulator for electrical wires because it does not conduct current well. The plastic casing allows people to touch the wires without getting shocked, and it prevents the current from flowing into objects that are touching the wires.

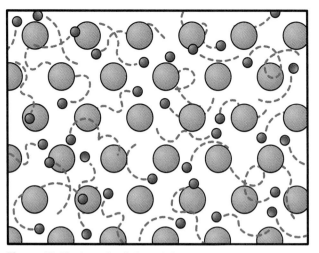 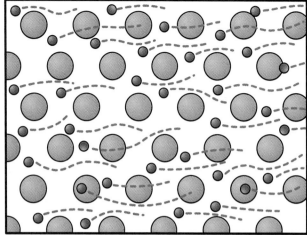

Figure 10: Electron clouds in metal

Note: Metals contain electrons that are not part of particular atoms (left). When current flows through metal (right), these electrons can flow like a liquid.

what can be described as an "electron cloud" that flows easily through the metal. When a voltage is applied to a metal or other conductor, these electrons move away from the negative area toward the positive area (see Figure 10). If a path is available for these electrons, they can even leave the conductor, provided other electrons are added in the negative area to replace them.

Insulators are made of atoms that have electrons that do not wander. These atoms hold their electrons more tightly. It takes a very high voltage to get their electrons to move from atom to atom. When this happens, the material is often damaged.

As you saw in Investigation 4, some liquids (but not all) are highly conductive. Pure compounds, including water and alcohol, do not conduct electricity well. The only pure liquids that have high conductivity are metals, such as mercury. However, when you tested salt water, you discovered that it *did* conduct current well. How can this be?

NO SALT, PLEASE

The answer is complicated. First of all, salt water is not a pure compound. It's a mixture, and some mixtures are better conductors than pure compounds. Second, you need to know that electrons do not travel through salt water. This means salt water must

contain other charged particles that *do* travel when current flows through it. The molecules of some compounds, including salt, are held together by electrical attraction between charged atoms or molecules. For example, salt (sodium chloride) is composed of the elements sodium and chlorine. Each sodium atom is missing one electron. (These atoms are positively charged.) Each chlorine atom has an extra electron. (These atoms are negatively charged.)

Insulators are made of atoms that have electrons that do not wander.

Atoms or molecules with an electrical charge are called **ions**. In compounds made of ions, such as salt crystals, the ions are held in a rigid three-dimensional pattern. But when ionic compounds dissolve in water, their ions separate and move randomly through the solution. Many nonionic compounds, such as sugar, can also dissolve in water, but their molecules do not break up into ions when they do.

Because ions can spread through a solution, when a pair of wires (conductors) with a difference in voltage between them are placed in a solution of ions, the negative ions will move toward positive areas in the solution and the positive ions will move toward negative areas in the solution. Once the ions reach the wires to which they are attracted, they either gain or lose electrons and they become other related substances. For example, positive copper ions will move toward a wire that is connected to the negative end of a battery. When these copper ions reach the negative wire, they accept electrons from the wire and become copper atoms. Eventually, a layer of copper metal builds up on the surface of the wire (see Figure 11).

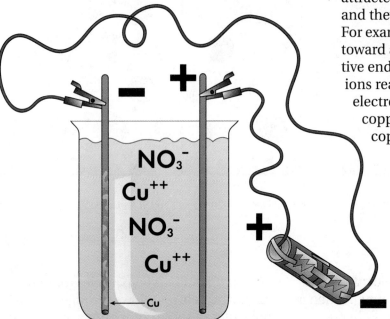

Figure 11: Ion migration

Note: Positive copper ions (Cu++) become neutral copper metal atoms (Cu) on the negative wire.

YOU ARE THE SOLUTION

Have you ever seen a solution of ions? You yourself are a solution of ions! Living cells consist mostly of water, with many things dissolved in it, including ions. It is not surprising that an electric current can run through your body or interfere with how it functions. An electric shock can cause a slight tingle, some

ALL CHARGED UP!

Suppose you turn on the TV one morning and you hear the weatherman say, "The air is going to be full of positive ions today." Would that news be positive or negative for your lungs?

And the answer is . . . negative.

In good, healthful, easy-to-breathe air, positive and negative ions are evenly distributed. But polluted air contains more positive ions than negative ones. Here's the reason:

The air is full of ions. A typical cubic centimeter of air contains from 1,000 to 2,000 of them. (This is just a tiny portion of the total number of molecules in the air.)

As water and other molecules in the air break apart, they release electrons. If a neutral molecule loses an electron, which has a negative charge, what remains of the molecule has a positive charge. If the released electron links up with a neutral molecule, this molecule will take on a negative charge. If the electron links up with a positively charged molecule, this molecule will become neutral.

Pollutants such as dust, smoke, car exhaust, and factory emissions bond with negative ions, reducing the negative charge in the air. Pollution is reduced when negative ions, such as hydroxyl (OH−), combine with these positive ions. This helps to remove the positive ions from the air.

Negative ions come from natural sources, such as oceans and waterfalls. Unfortunately, there is so much pollution in the air today that this natural process cannot keep all the air clean, especially around busy streets and industrial areas.

If this bird decides to hop onto the wire, it will not be electrocuted. The bird's claws would be in contact with only a small portion of the wire, and so there would be no difference in voltage on its legs. Therefore, current would not flow through the bird.

discomfort, or death, depending on the amount of the electric current and the path of the current.

If an electric shock sent current flowing through your heart, it would be extremely dangerous because your heart is regulated by electrical impulses. The more current that passes through the heart, the greater the danger. How much current would be life-threatening? A 60-watt lightbulb uses about one-half (0.5) ampere. About 0.02 amperes can kill you. A current of 0.004 amperes is uncomfortable to most people.

To avoid being shocked, you must never come in contact with two conductors that are at different voltages, such as the side and base of a plugged-in lightbulb socket. If you do, your body will complete a circuit and current will flow through you.

GROUNDED

You may have noticed that some electrical devices, such as air conditioners, have three wires, not just the two needed to complete a circuit. Inside the machine, this third wire is connected to the metal frame. Outside the machine, this wire is connected to the third prong of the electric plug. When plugged in, the third prong connects with another wire that is attached to a pipe or other conductor that runs deep into the ground. If current ever leaks through a break in the electrical insulation and electrifies the frame of the appliance, it will run through the third wire into the ground. This helps prevent shocks to anyone who touches the appliance. Because the planet Earth is so large, it can easily absorb or release electrons. Any slight charge it acquires is spread over a large area and is hardly noticeable. The practice of connecting electrical devices to the earth is called **grounding**.

Grounding is a way of removing excess charge. A bird that perches on a high-voltage line does not get a shock even if some current leaks through a worn-out insulator. The bird's claws touch only a small portion of the wire, and so there is no difference in voltage on its legs. If there is

GET THIS . . .

Ions are atoms or molecules with an electrical charge.

no difference in voltage, current will not flow through the bird. But if one of the bird's wings would happen to touch a metal pole supporting the wire, then the bird would become part of the grounding path. Current would flow through the bird, which would probably be electrocuted.

Power lines are extremely dangerous. You should never work or play near power lines. If you were moving a ladder to paint a house and the ladder came in contact with a power line, current would shoot through the ladder and your body into the ground, and you could be fatally injured.

ON YOUR OWN

Answer the following questions based on "Electrical Conductivity (and Safe Conduct)."

1 How would you explain the fact that pure water does not conduct electricity well?

2 How would you explain that solid crystals of salt do not conduct electricity well, though salt dissolved in water does?

3 What is dangerous about using a fork to remove a piece of bread that is stuck in a toaster? What would be a safe way to remove it?

4 Many electricians work with one hand behind the back or in a pocket. What might be the reason for this?

Some Metals Are More Active Than Others

EVER WONDER?

Why are most electrical wires made with copper? You have already learned that metals are good conductors of electricity. So why is copper more popular than aluminum or steel when it comes to making wires? You have probably seen many buildings that have aluminum siding. Did you ever wonder why buildings don't have siding made of other metals? And why does iron rust so easily, while aluminum and "stainless steel" do not?

In this investigation you will explore some of the differences among metals and will begin to see what causes those differences.

MATERIALS LIST

- Lemon or other citrus fruit
- Strips of various metals
- Steel wool
- 2 wires with alligator clips (20 cm long)
- Small lightbulb with bulb holder or wires attached
- Voltmeter (optional)
- Zinc nitrate solution
- Copper nitrate solution
- Magnesium nitrate solution
- Iron nitrate solution
- 4 beakers (25 mL)
- Plastic gloves
- Safety goggles

STEP-BY-STEP

1 Set up a data table in your logbook. The table should be similar to the following sample, but you will need six blank rows, not just two.

Metal 1	Metal 2	Bulb	Voltage

2 Put on your safety goggles.

3 Stick the zinc strip into the lemon near one end of the fruit.

4 Insert the copper strip near the other end of the lemon. Record the names of the two metals in the first two columns of your data table.

5 Attach a separate wire to each metal strip. Use alligator clips to make the attachments.

6 Attach the other ends of the wires to the lightbulb. Observe the bulb, and record your observations in the third column of your table.

7 Remove the bulb, and connect the two wires to the voltmeter. Record the voltage in the fourth column of the table.

8 Remove the zinc and copper strips from the fruit. Throughout this investigation, every time that you remove a metal strip be sure to rinse it thoroughly with water and then dry it.

9 Using a different pair of metal strips, repeat Steps 3–8.

10 Continue repeating the procedure until all six possible pairs of metals have been tested.

11 Set up a data table in your logbook: List your metal samples down the left side of the table, and list your solutions across the top.

12 Label each of four beakers with the name of the solution that it will contain.

13 Wearing protective gloves, pour about 5–10 mL of each solution into its beaker.

14 Use steel wool to polish each strip of metal so that it is bright and shiny. *Caution: Be careful not to cut your fingers on the edges of the metal strips.*

15 Place each strip of metal into the solution that has the same "first name." For example, put the copper strip in the copper nitrate solution.

16 Observe for two or three minutes. Then record your observations in your data table: For each combination of a metal and a solution that react, place "R" in the corresponding row and column; for each combination of a metal and a solution that do not react, place "NR" in the appropriate row and column.

17 Remove the metal strips, and rinse them well with water. Repolish the strips with steel wool, as in Step 14.

18 Now place each strip in a different solution.

19 Observe for two or three minutes. Record your observations.

20 Repeat Steps 17–19 until every metal has been in every solution. Record your observations after each test.

21 Follow your teacher's instructions for cleaning up your work area and for storing materials.

CAREER LINKS

Engineering Technologies

GEOPHYSICIST

Oil, uranium, gold, titanium, and many other valuable resources lie within the earth. Geophysicists develop detailed maps and data to provide information about where these resources are located and how they can be tapped. Geological data are also useful to builders and planners who must decide where to erect new structures and where to locate landfills and hazardous-waste sites. To become a geophysicist, you will need a bachelor of science degree in geophysics or geology. If you want to rise to the managerial level, you will need a master of science or a Ph.D. degree. For further information about career opportunities in this field, write:

Geological Society of America
P.O. Box 9140
Boulder, CO 80301
http://www.geosociety.org

Related occupations: mining surveyor, petroleum and natural-gas engineer, meteorologist, environmental specialist, geochemist

TALK IT OVER

Collaborate with your partner(s) to answer these questions:

1. How did current move through the fruit? Did it travel as a stream of electrons or in some other form?

2. What are the characteristics of metals that allow them to conduct current? How might metals differ from one another in these characteristics?

3. How could differences between two metals cause current to flow from one to the other? (Hint: Think about a tug-of-war.)

4. What might be the energy source that caused the current to flow? Was the fruit the power source, or was it just a conductor that completed a circuit?

5. Do some metals react more easily than others? How could the differences you observed when you placed the metals in solutions be related to the differences you observed when you placed the metals in fruit?

6. Is it possible to rank the metals in the order of how easily they reacted? In what order would you rank them?

7. Compare the amount of voltage that each pair of metals generated with its rank in your list from Question 2. Is there any connection? What do your results have to do with electricity?

SPREAD THE WORD

Before preparing a presentation, discuss your results with the other member(s) of your team and with other teams. If interpretations differ, redo those parts of the investigation that led to your different conclusions. When your team reaches agreement on an interpretation of its results, prepare to report these results as follows:

First, prepare a large poster to show the rest of the class. This poster should include some sample metal strips that illustrate the types of results you obtained. Sketches of the strips illustrating any coating that formed would also be useful. Next, create a handout and make copies for everyone in the class. The handout should contain a list of the metals that you used in decreasing order of activity. (List the most active metal first, then the second most active, and so on.) Leave room on the handout for your listeners to write additional information about your results.

Finally, give an oral presentation. Describe what you did and what you think your results mean. Be sure to explain what you think is the connection between the electrical behavior of metals and the ability of metals to react with solutions of other metal ions. Also describe some ways that your ideas may be useful at home or at work. Discuss some types of jobs that would require an understanding of the connection between chemical reactions and electric currents.

READ ALL ABOUT IT!

Different Metals React in Different Ways

In Steps 1–10 of Investigation 5, you saw that an electric current will flow when two different metals are electrically connected by the ionic solution inside a lemon or some other piece of fruit. Earlier you learned that current (in the form of electrons) travels through metals and that current (in the form of ions) travels through solutions. But what made a current flow through the lemon? And why did some metals produce more current than others when they were attached to the fruit?

Steps 11–20 of the investigation provided a big clue that will help you answer these questions. As you learned from the 16 trials you conducted, some metals enter chemical reactions more easily than others. Remember, metals give up electrons fairly easily and become positive ions. Positive metal ions can also gain electrons, becoming neutral metal atoms. (Note: There is no such thing as a negative metal ion. Neutral metal atoms cannot gain electrons to become negative ions; however, some other kinds of substances *can* do this.)

HOLDING TIGHT

In the reactions you observed in Steps 11–20, one metal replaced another in solution. This means two things: The metal atoms of the strip became positive ions in solution, and the metal ions in solution became metal atoms. The fact that a coating formed was an indication that this process was occurring. But it did not occur easily in every case. Why not? Because some metals hold their electrons more tightly than others do. For example, copper tends to hold onto its electrons more tightly than iron does. Copper ions in a solution around a piece of iron tend to steal away some electrons from the atoms of the solid iron. The copper ions form a layer of neutral copper metal on the surface of the piece of iron, while iron atoms on the surface of the metal become ions and dissolve in the solution (see Figure 12). The reverse reaction—iron ions trading places with atoms of solid copper—does not occur so easily.

A layer of copper or other metal can be made to coat the surface of a metal object

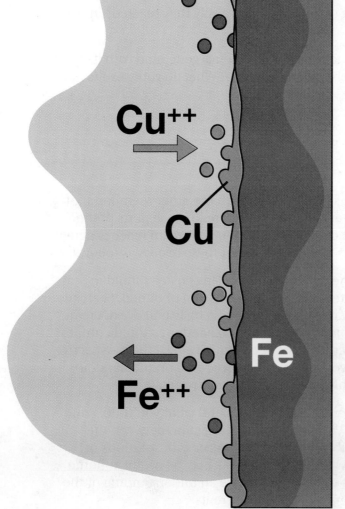

Figure 12: Ion exchange at metal surface
Note: Iron atoms can donate electrons to copper ions. The iron atoms become iron ions, and the copper ions become copper atoms.

Jumpin' Frog Legs!

What is inside animals that makes it possible for them to move? An Italian doctor named Luigi Galvani thought the answer was that all living creatures have some kind of electricity inside them. In 1786 he came up with evidence that supported his theory.

When Galvani touched a dead frog's legs with a pair of scissors, the legs suddenly twitched. He suspected that the frog's muscles had reacted to a current of electricity from the scissors. He conducted more tests by applying direct current to the muscles and nerves of several frogs. For Galvani, these experiments demonstrated that the fluids inside organisms were electrical.

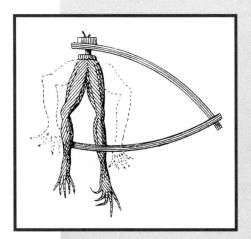

Around the same time, Alessandro Volta, a physicist, was also experimenting with frogs and electricity. Like Galvani, he discovered that a frog's legs would contract when they were touched with a metal probe; however, he had another explanation for this effect. According to Volta, electricity is a powerful force that affects anything through which it passes, including live and dead organisms. For Volta, the fact that a dead frog's tissue jumps when a current is applied to it merely indicates the power of electricity.

Both Galvani and Volta were partially right because the connections in an animal's nervous system are electrical in nature.

Today's scientists have a much better understanding of how nerve cells build up and discharge electrical potentials.

---

more quickly if a voltage is applied to the solution and the metal object. This process, which is called **electroplating**, is used to create the surface layer of silver or gold on such things as silver-plated eating utensils and gold-plated jewelry.

The tendency of electrons to move from one metal to another . . . is called the Galvanic effect.

When you placed two different metal strips in the fruit, one of them attracted electrons more strongly than the other one did. Electrons traveled through the wire and bulb from one metal to the other. As more charge built up in one metal strip than the other, a difference in voltage resulted. This caused ions in the fruit to move from one strip to the other, completing a circuit. The tendency of electrons to move from one metal to another, where they will be more strongly held, is called the **Galvanic effect**.

Oxidation Again

You may have learned that oxidation means reaction with oxygen. Now that you have learned about electrons and ions, you can understand oxidation in a more advanced way: **Oxidation** is the process in which a substance loses electrons. The opposite of oxidation is called reduction. **Reduction** is the process in which a substance gains electrons. Positive ions that gain electrons and become neutral are being reduced. In the reactions with oxygen that you have known as oxidations, the fuel that is oxidized loses electrons, while the oxygen that is involved in the reaction gains electrons and becomes reduced.

Metals can be listed in a series in which each metal can reduce any metal ion that is below it in the series. See Figure 13 for a list of some of the more common metals in their order of reactivity. This kind of list is called an **electromotive series**.

Element	Symbol	
Lithium	Li	*most reactive, easy to oxidize (loses electrons easily)*
Potassium	K	
Calcium	Ca	
Sodium	Na	
Magnesium	Mg	
Aluminum	Al	
Zinc	Zn	
Iron	Fe	
Nickel	Ni	
Tin	Sn	
Lead	Pb	
Copper	Cu	
Mercury	Hg	
Silver	Ag	
Gold	Au	*least reactive, hard to oxidize (holds electrons tightly)*

Figure 13: An electromotive series

ON YOUR OWN

Answer the following questions based on "Different Metals React in Different Ways."

1 How would you explain the unpleasant feeling that occurs when a metal spoon or fork touches a metal dental filling?

2 What is probably the reason that the part of an earring that goes through a person's ear is usually made of "surgical gold"?

3 What might be the reason that steel roofs and trash cans are often coated with a layer of zinc?

Science L i n k s

Electric Language

EVER WONDER?

How many languages do you speak? English? Spanish? Chinese? Italian? Electric? . . . You may not realize it, but you communicate in "Electric" every day. Whenever you use a telephone, TV, or computer and every time you listen to recorded music, you are using electricity to send or receive information that can be converted into sound or pictures.

How do people use electricity to communicate? How do sounds and pictures travel through wires and cables? In this investigation you will discover how electricity moves information from one place to another.

MATERIALS LIST

- Flashlight
- Graph paper
- Watch or clock with second hand (optional)

STEP-BY-STEP

1. Choose three members of your group to work together on Step 2 while the fourth member completes Step 3.

2. Develop a system of light flashes for sending and receiving information. Decide what each flash or series of flashes will mean. You will be using your system to transmit information that will be used to reconstruct a picture made out of black and white squares on graph paper. Continue with Step 4.

3. Create an image of some kind on a 10x10 square area of a piece of graph paper by filling in some squares completely and leaving other squares blank. Do not let anyone else see your image at this time. Continue with Step 4.

4. Two group members who have not seen the image that was created in Step 3 should move on to Step 5 while the other two members complete Step 6.

5. Sit across the room from the other pair of group members. Draw a frame around a 10x10 square area of a piece of graph paper. One of you will have the task of watching the light flashes and calling them out, while the other one will have to write down the information as it is called out. Tell the other pair when you are ready to receive the message. Continue with Step 7.

6. Use the "code" developed in Step 2 to write down the sequence of flashes that you will need to send the message of the image. Continue with Step 8.

Current Thoughts

7 As the message is sent, record the flashes. When the message ends, use the information that you received to reconstruct the image in your 10x10 frame. When you are finished, join the other two group members and compare pictures.

8 Use the flashlight to transmit your image to the pair across the room. Do not communicate with them in any other way about the information you are sending. They will try to reconstruct the image. When they are finished, they will check with you to compare pictures.

9 The two pairs should now switch roles. Those who received the first message should draw a new picture and send it to the pair who sent the first one. Reconstruct the second picture, and see if it is accurate.

TALK IT OVER

Work with the other members of your group on the following items.

1 Explain how the code that you used in flashing the light could also be used to send information through a wire with electricity.

2 In the system you used, what would happen to the message if a single flash of information were not received? Suppose some kind of "interference" broke up your transmission—would all the rest of the message be confused, or would only a certain portion of it be messed up? What did you do (or what could you do) to limit the effect of a brief interruption?

3 How could you use an on-and-off code, such as light flashes, to transmit words?

SPREAD THE WORD

Prepare a presentation describing how you carried out this investigation. Tell what you learned about encoding, transmitting, and receiving information. You could demonstrate how your system works by sending a message so that the whole class can receive and interpret it. Describe at least two different systems that you could use to encode and send information, and compare their advantages and disadvantages.

List at least three types of workers who could use this knowledge. For each worker, tell who is communicating with whom and how the information is transmitted.

COPY CHARGES

Have you ever thought about how a copying machine works? Is making a photocopy the same thing as taking a picture with a camera? As a matter of fact, photocopying involves magnetism and electricity more than photography.

Inside the copying machine is a rotating plate that is coated with a light-sensitive material, such as selenium. The plate is charged with static electricity. When you copy a document, the original is scanned and light is reflected from the original onto the charged plate. The dark areas (words and pictures) of the original form a positively charged image on the plate.

The plate then is dusted with toner (ink powder). Because the toner is negatively charged, it sticks to the positively charged image areas on the plate, and the plate becomes negatively charged. The paper that is used to make copies is positively charged; therefore, the negatively charged image on the plate is transferred to the paper. Finally, heat is applied to bond the particles to the paper.

Making a copy is a matter of trading charges.

READ ALL ABOUT IT!

Coded Messages

COMPUTERS are great for writing papers and playing video games, but do you know how a computer actually works? How does a computer turn your keystrokes into letters and numbers? And what does the coded message that you sent with a flashlight in the previous investigation have to do with computers?

All electrical devices, including the circuits inside computers, can exist in only two states: They are either "on" or "off." In computer code, these two states are represented as "1" (current or voltage is on) and "0" (current or voltage is off). By switching on and off very quickly, the tiny circuits of a computer can use these two states to represent every letter, number, and punctuation mark in anything you key.

These two symbols—1 and 0—are not enough to represent all the letters and numbers that people need to communicate with one another. The men and women who program computers solve this problem by using more than one 0 or 1 for each letter, number, or punctuation mark. Because numbers (digits) are used to represent information, this system is called a **digital code**.

THINK OF THE POSSIBILITIES

There are four possible two-digit codes: 00, 01, 10, and 11; therefore, two digits are enough to represent four different letters of the alphabet. Three digits can represent eight letters; four digits can represent 16; five letters can represent 32, and so on. It turns out that eight-digit codes provide enough combinations for all the letters, numbers, and other symbols on a computer keyboard, as well as all other programming operations. For example, the code 01000001 stands for A, and 01001101 stands for M.

The keys on a computer keyboard are actually switches. When you press a key, it completes a circuit that sends a signal to the computer in the form of a series of brief pulses of current. Each pulse lasts a certain amount of time. An interval when a pulse is sent counts as a 1. An interval when no pulse is sent counts as a 0. Computers can send and receive these pulses extremely fast; therefore, many 0s and 1s can be sent every second. These 0s and 1s are known as **bits** of information

This is how all electronic communication circuits work, whether they involve a computer connection to the Internet, a long-distance telephone conversation with your grandmother, or a fax that you send to order a pizza.

Answer the following questions based on "Coded Messages."

1 How can all the colors and shapes in a television picture be represented in a digital code? (Hint: Look closely at a television or computer screen to see how the picture is formed.)

2 Which is likely to be more accurate, a number reported in digital code or a reading on a needle gauge, such as a speedometer? Explain your answer.

3 What limits how much digital information a computer can send per minute?

SECTION WRAP-UP

Keep an Eye on Those Ions

Y OU'RE just about to brush your teeth when you notice a large green stain on the bathroom floor. You check the hot and cold water lines under the sink. Neither one of them is leaking. So you turn on the water to see what happens. There— as the water gurgles down the drain, it begins trickling out of the U-shaped drainpipe at the point where two sections of pipe are joined.

You notice that the two pieces of pipe are different. One is copper, and the other is some silvery-gray metal. The green stains caused by the dripping water tell you what has happened: When your Uncle Larry did your parents a "favor" by installing a new sink last summer, he connected two different kinds of metal. The difference in voltage between them has caused a current to flow.

PLUMBING LESSON

You remember the green copper salt solution that you saw in your science class. The green stain on the floor must be caused by copper ions from some chemical

reaction between the two metals and the water in the pipe. The reaction between the metals slowly corroded the joint between them until water began to leak out. Uncle Larry meant well, but your parents would have been better off with a real plumber.

Your science knowledge comes to the rescue. You know that the metal atoms in the pipe do not hold their outer electrons tightly. The reaction that caused the corrosion occurred because electrons flowed from one of the metals (the one that held them less tightly) to the other. Once some of those atoms started to lose electrons and become ions, it was easy for them to dissolve in the water in the pipe and spill out onto the floor.

As you wipe up the mess and place a plastic bowl under the pipe, you realize how lucky you were to spot it. You were standing there in your bare feet, and you were about to use your electric toothbrush. Any current that leaked out into your hand from the brush would have gone right through your salty body fluids. Just to be on the safe side, you decide to put on your slippers with the rubber soles before you brush your teeth.

As soon as you tell your mom about the leak—and the danger—she gets on the phone and calls Peggy's A-1 Plumbing. As she speaks, her voice produces voltage in the microphone, and the phone converts this voltage into a series of quick, identical pulses of current. These pulses travel over the phone wires to the plumber's phone, where they are decoded and converted back into sounds by the speaker in the receiver.

It's all set. Tomorrow you will have a new drainpipe made of just one material, plastic. No more electrical chemistry under the sink. You look at your watch. You really wanted to relax in the tub, but your favorite TV show is about to start. For a moment you think about taking your portable TV into the bathroom and watching it there. No way! A high-voltage picture tube and a tub full of tap water (and mineral ions) could end in disaster.

ON YOUR OWN

Answer the following questions based on "Keep an Eye on Those Ions."

1 How would plastic plumbing prevent electrical corrosion? How is plastic different from metal? What other effects would plastic pipes have on electrical safety?

2 What are some ways that the electric toothbrush in the story could be made safe?

3 Is the high voltage of a TV set necessary for it to use digital code, or does the high voltage have some other purpose?

CAREER LINKS

AEROSPACE ENGINEER

If you want a career in a high-tech field of the future, you may want to think about aerospace engineering. The men and women who ride rockets into space depend on engineers to design, build, and maintain many essential systems, from communications to onboard power units. To design solar panels and other electrical systems for astronauts, you will need at least a bachelor's degree in engineering. Engineering school is difficult, but it is a doorway to an interesting and rewarding career. Because of the high level of mathematical and scientific knowledge required in this field, it would be a good idea to plan on continuing your education after earning the B.S. degree. For more information, write:

American Institute of Aeronautics and Astronautics
1801 Alexander Bell Drive, Suite 500
Reston, VA 20191-4344
http://www.aiaa.org

Related occupations: Propulsion specialist, navigation engineer, aircraft designer, guidance systems developer

Engineering Technologies

ATTRACTION AND REPULSION

DID you ever wonder what makes a compass point north? What is it about the earth that causes compasses to indicate one direction or another? Is it some kind of force? Do compasses and other magnets have anything to do with the force of electricity?

All the electrical energy that you use comes from somewhere. How does it get started? Is there some kind of machine that "makes" electricity? How does burning coal or running water over a dam let the electric company produce a voltage to power your lights and TV?

In this section you will explore these questions in much the same way as the scientists who originally asked them. Using compasses, magnets, and lightbulbs, you will uncover the hidden forces of magnetism and electricity. And you will learn how the links between these basic forces enable some of the world's most important inventions to operate.

FREEZE FRAME

Now that you have seen the video segment, discuss the following on-screen questions with the other students in your class.

1 How can computers use electricity to store information in the form of tiny magnetized zones?

2 How is the relationship between electricity and magnetism used to produce energy?

Magnetic Attraction

EVER WONDER?

The needle of a compass points toward the north. Have you ever wondered how it "knows" where north is? Do all compasses have the same things inside them? If you took a compass apart, what would you find inside?

To learn the answers to these questions, in this investigation you will experiment with the different ways compasses work. You will also discover some "hidden properties" of magnets.

MATERIALS LIST

- Compass
- Bar magnet
- Rocks of different kinds and sizes
- Radio
- Pieces of wood
- Pieces of metal
- Meter stick

STEP-BY-STEP

1 Hold the compass a few centimeters from the magnet. Observe which end of the compass needle points to the north pole of the magnet. Record your finding in your logbook.

2 Hold the compass against the magnet, and stand facing the north pole. Then move the compass back a half-centimeter at a time: 0.5 cm, 1.0 cm, 1.5 cm, 2.0 cm, 2.5 cm, etc. Record in your logbook how the compass reacts at each of these distances. (Continue moving the compass until the magnet no longer has an effect on it.)

3 Repeat the procedure you followed in Step 2, but this time start with the compass touching the south pole of the magnet. Again record your observations in your logbook.

4 Slowly move the compass from one end of the magnet to the other. Then move the compass up, down, and sideways from the middle of the magnet. Record your observations.

5 Test other items in the room to see how they affect the compass needle. Try different kinds of things, such as rocks, a radio, pieces of wood, etc. List the items that you test, and record how the compass reacts to each one. Also note the distance at which each item begins to affect the compass.

6 Use the compass to determine the shape of the magnetic field around the magnet. In your logbook draw a diagram of the magnet and its field.

7 In your diagram, label the north and south poles of the magnet (use the letters "N" and "S"). Also label the areas of the magnet that had a high, medium, or low effect on the compass (use the letters "H," "M," and "L").

TALK IT OVER

Work with the other members of your group to answer the following questions.

1 How does the influence of the magnet on the compass change with distance?

2 Does the influence of the magnet on the compass seem stronger in certain places (standing next to particular sides) rather than other places? What are the strongest areas of influence?

3 What, if anything, do you think might block or reduce the effect of the magnet on the compass?

CAREER LINKS

Mechanics & Transportation

U.S. Department of Defense

AIRCRAFT MECHANIC

Every day giant jetliners carry hundreds of passengers to their destinations throughout the world. The mechanics who inspect and repair the engines and other equipment on these planes are responsible for the safety of all those people. Aircraft mechanics use electronic and magnetic devices to determine if engine and other systems are working properly. One way to get started in this field is to get on-the-job training through a technical school. The Federal Aviation Administration (FAA) certifies technicians to work on aircraft. FAA certification depends on experience in different types of repair. Someone without certification may work under the supervision of an aircraft mechanic to obtain experience. Courses in physics, electronics, computer science, and drafting provide a strong educational background. For more information, write:

Professional Aviation Maintenance Association
1200 18th Street, N.W., Suite 401
Washington, DC 20036-2506
http://www.pama.org

Related occupations: maintenance mechanic, aircraft inspector, electronic automechanics specialist

PERSONAL MAGNETISM

How do animals find their way over great distances? Tiny hummingbirds migrate from one continent to another, returning to the same winter and summer homes year after year. Giant sea turtles swim thousands of kilometers through the ocean to nest on the very beaches where they were born. Sharks follow long-distance underwater routes that are as precise as the flight paths of jet planes. . . .

Many people think birds navigate by using rivers and landmarks, as well as the sun, moon, and stars. But if that's all birds do to find their way, how do they keep from getting lost on foggy days and cloudy nights? Do they have to stop flying till the weather improves?

Although scientists are not completely sure how animals navigate, the most likely explanation is that they rely mostly on the direction and strength of the earth's magnetic field. Their brains and bodies have "magnetoreceptors," which are like built-in compasses that respond to the planet's magnetic field.

The magnetic field at the earth's surface is weak; it has only one-thousandth the strength of the field that a refrigerator magnet produces. But animals' magnetoreceptors are extremely sensitive. Researchers have discovered that sharks, rays, newts, and some insects can detect tiny changes in the direction and strength of magnetic fields. The internal compasses of animals may be the best navigational instruments in the world.

RESULTS SPREAD THE WORD

Work with your group to plan a presentation of your findings. Use the data you obtained during the investigation to create a large chart showing the magnet and the various levels and ranges of influence around it. Draw lines connecting the regions of high influence around the magnet, and describe any patterns you see in these areas. To help other students see how the pattern of a magnetic field looks, you could sprinkle iron filings on a sheet of paper and hold a magnet under the sheet.

Describe how the reaction of the compass to the magnet differed from its reaction to the other items you examined. Also tell whether these other objects influenced the compass in the same way that the magnet did. Was the pattern of influence the same, considering distance and strength?

Explain to the class how you could use a compass and a map to find your way on a hike through the woods. Finally, discuss some everyday activities or jobs in which knowledge of magnetic fields is useful.

It's a Magnetic World

ANCIENT sailors used to hang a large piece of lodestone—the same kind of mineral that you used during Investigation 7—in the front of their ships. When they could not see any landmarks or stars, the only way they could tell where they were heading was to watch how the lodestone positioned itself. The stone always faced north.

Today sailors use a compass to navigate on the high seas, but the principle behind the compass is the same principle that is behind the lodestone. The earth is a gigantic magnet whose range of influence, or **magnetic field**, extends from below the surface to high in the atmosphere. A "field" is an area in which an object experiences a certain force. (The strength of the force depends on the location of the object.) In a magnetic field, the force is strongest near the two poles of the magnet. When a magnetic substance, such as lodestone, is free to move, it will position itself according to this magnetic field. The north end of a magnet or lodestone will point toward the **magnetic north** pole of the earth.

TRUE OR FALSE?
Magnetic north is not the same as **true north**, which is the

actual geographic location of the north pole, the northernmost point of the earth's **axis**. (You probably already know that this axis is an imaginary line that runs through the center of the earth from the north pole to the south pole and that the earth spins on its axis.) How far east or west magnetic north is from true north depends on the location of the person who does the measuring.

From any point on the surface of the earth, if you draw one line that extends to the true north pole and another line that extends to the magnetic north pole, the size of the angle formed by these two lines is called the angle of **magnetic declination**. If you connect all the surface points that have the same declination, you produce a curve called an **isogonic line**. If you could see all the isogonic lines on the surface of the earth, you would see that they resemble the lines of force you mapped around the magnet during the investigation (see Figure 14).

SQUIGGLES IN THE LINES
Have you ever wondered how explorers find shipwrecks and lost treasures at the bottom of the ocean? Any squiggles in the isogonic lines indicate that something is creating a

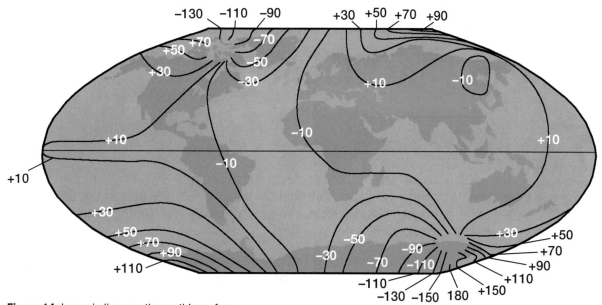

Figure 14: Isogonic lines on the earth's surface
Note: The numbers represent the magnetic declination in degrees along each line.

magnetic field that is interfering with the magnetic field of the earth. **Magnetometers** are sensitive compasses that detect these magnetic fluctuations. They are used on planes and ships to locate man-made metallic objects and large deposits of minerals. Concentrations of metallic minerals, such as lodestone, might produce isogonic squiggles.

What causes the earth's magnetic field? Scientists are not certain, but the answer seems to be that the field is caused by the concentration of strongly magnetic materials, such as iron and nickel, in the earth's core. Heat and the rotation of the planet cause the iron-rich material in the core to circulate slowly. The movement of molten metals within the earth produces slow changes in the positions of the planet's magnetic poles. When magnetic material solidifies, it preserves the orientation of the earth's magnetic field at that time; therefore, rocks with different orientations serve as evidence that the poles have shifted over time.

Magnetometers on spacecraft can reveal detailed information about magnetism on the earth and other planets. This information has provided valuable clues to the structure and history of the earth, moon, and solar system.

ON YOUR OWN

Respond to the following items based on "It's a Magnetic World."

1 Magnets are often marked "N" and "S" to show which pole is north and which one is south. Is the earth's north magnetic pole a pole of north or south magnetism? Explain your answer.

2 Describe how an isogonic map could help you use your compass if you went hiking in a region for the first time.

3 You may have seen people on beaches using metal detectors to locate valuables in the sand. Could a magnetometer be used as a metal detector? Explain.

Current Thoughts

Plug in That Magnet

EVER WONDER?

If you're like most students, you can't wait to get your own car. But most people don't know very much about how cars work. They may know that a generator and an electric starter motor are under the hood, but they probably can't explain how these devices are related.

Both a motor and a generator produce energy, but do they produce it the same way? Are a generator and a motor related in any other way? And does either one of them use magnets to produce energy? In this investigation you will learn the answers to these questions as you explore the relationship between magnetism and electricity.

MATERIALS LIST

- Piece of wire
- Spool of wire
- Lantern battery
- Small lightbulb
- Compass
- Bar magnet
- Safety goggles

STEP-BY-STEP (PART 1)

1 Put on your safety goggles.

2 Wrap a piece of wire around the compass two times. Line up the wire with the north-south markings of the compass.

3 Connect the ends of the wire to the battery terminals (see Figure 15).

4 Observe how the compass reacts. Record your observations in your logbook.

5 Reverse the connections: Disconnect the wire that was connected to the negative (–) terminal, and connect it to the positive (+) terminal; disconnect the wire that was connected to the positive terminal, and connect it to the negative terminal.

6 Observe how the compass reacts, and record your observations.

7 Disconnect the wire from the battery.

8 Wrap the wire around the compass twice, but this time line it up in an east-west direction.

9 Connect the ends of the wire to the battery terminals, and record the results in your logbook.

10 Reverse the connections, as you did in Step 5. When both ends of the wire are again connected to the terminals, record any changes that you observe in the compass.

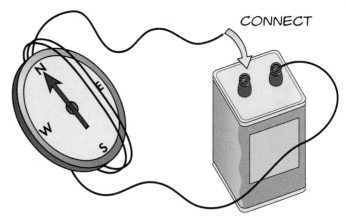

CONNECT

Figure 15: Equipment setup for Investigation 8, Part 1

11 Disconnect the wire from the battery.

12 Wrap the wire around the compass 10 times in a north-south direction.

13 Connect the wire to the battery terminals, and record your observations in your logbook.

STEP-BY-STEP (PART 2)

1 Expose and strip the insulation off both ends of the wire on the spool, if this has not been done already. Do not remove the wire from the spool.

2 Attach the ends of the wire to the bulb or socket.

3 Hold the magnet by one end and push it quickly back and forth through the coiled wire (see Figure 16). Observe what happens, and record the results in your logbook.

MOTION

4 Turn the magnet around so that you are now holding it by the other end. Move it quickly through the coiled wire loops. Note the results in your logbook.

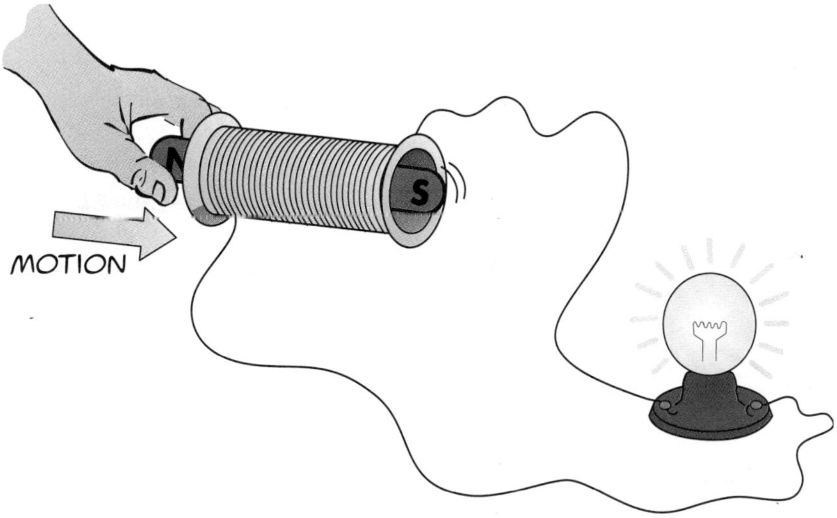

Figure 16: Equipment setup for Investigation 8, Part 2

5 Return all materials according to your teacher's instructions.

Current Thoughts

TALK IT OVER

Work with your partner to answer the following questions.

1 Does the current flowing through the wire influence the magnetic field near the compass needle? Describe how this works.

2 Did the number of times the wire was wrapped around the compass affect the movement of the compass needle? Does electric current produce a magnetic field? Explain.

3 Did the motion of the magnet create an electric current? Explain.

4 How could the relationship between electricity and magnetism be used to produce electric power?

SPREAD THE WORD

Work with your partner to present your findings to the rest of the class. As you talk about each part of the investigation, explain which variables you think were important and which ones seemed to make no difference. Be sure to explain how the investigation shows that electricity and magnetism are related and how they affect each other. Mention some devices or equipment that depend on this relationship. Also list ways in which the relationship between electricity and magnetism could be useful in a career that you might like to pursue.

SUPERCONDUCTORS

Every time an electric current is transmitted through a material, it faces resistance. In overcoming the resistance, the current loses some of its energy.

Scientists are trying to develop materials that will carry electricity more efficiently. They are even trying to develop "superconductors," materials that offer no resistance to current. If superconducting power lines can be developed, electrical current could be transmitted over great distances without losing any energy.

Finding materials that will work as superconductors has turned out to be a difficult task. The main problem is temperature: Metals and alloys do not superconduct until their temperature is near absolute zero (–273.15°C). Ceramic materials can superconduct at temperatures around –180°C.

Scientists are searching for materials that will superconduct at much higher temperatures. Because the known superconductors work only at extremely cold temperatures, there are not many everyday applications for them. Today superconductivity is being used mainly in scientific research, such as experiments that require a great amount of power to be maintained at a steady level.

READ ALL ABOUT IT!

Current Attractions . . . and Repulsions

THE trials that you conducted in Investigation 8 are similar to what scientists did in the early nineteenth century when they discovered the relationship between magnetism and electricity. While exploring how various metals react to electric current, H.C. Oersted placed a magnet below a circuit wire and discovered that the magnet positioned itself perpendicular to the flow of current. When he put the magnet above the wire, it turned perpendicular to the current flow, but in the opposite direction. From these results, Oersted concluded that electric current produces a magnetic field.

Michael Faraday wanted to find out if this relationship worked the other way around. In much the same way that you did, Faraday built a circuit with coiled wire and moved a magnet up and down inside the coil. This generated an electric current. Further experimentation showed that an electric current could also be produced by holding the magnet still and moving the wires up and down around it. It became clear that a moving electric current produces a magnetic field and that a moving or changing magnetic field produces electric current.

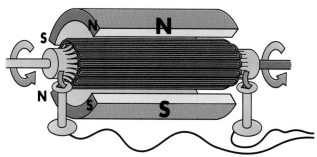

Figure 17: Simplified view inside a generator
Note: As the coiled wire spins between the poles of the magnet, a current is generated in the wire.

POWER SPIN

Many devices that people use every day are based on the relationship between electricity and magnetism. Whenever a magnet is spun around inside a coil of wire (or vice versa), an electric current begins to flow in the wire (see Figure 17). This current can be used right away, as when you flick on a light switch, or it can be collected and stored for later use, as in a car battery. A **generator** uses this principle to convert mechanical energy to electrical energy. An alternator in a car is a type of generator that uses some of the power of the car's engine to produce electric power to recharge the car's battery as the vehicle is being driven. Electric power plants use a variety of energy resources to operate huge generators.

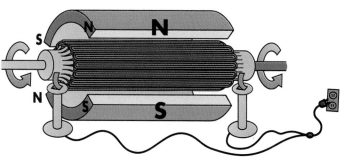

Figure 18: Simplified view inside a motor
Note: Current flowing through the coiled wire creates a magnetic field that repels the magnet outside, causing the coil and shaft to spin.

An electric motor applies this principle in reverse. Motors contain a coiled wire and a magnet. One of these is mounted on the inside of the cover of the motor, and the other is on the shaft. When electric current flows through the coil, the magnetic fields of the coil and the magnet repel each other, causing the shaft to spin (see Figure 18). Motors are used to power fans, blenders, refrigerators, washing machines, drills, and an enormous number of other devices.

ON YOUR OWN

Respond to the following items based on "Current Attractions . . . and Repulsions."

1 Describe why more coils in a current-carrying wire might produce a stronger magnetic field.

2 Suppose you are driving along in a car, using a car compass to find your way. The compass shows that you are heading steadily east; then all of a sudden it begins spinning like crazy. What could be the reason for this? What nearby object or material might cause the compass to act this way? Explain your answer.

3 Give five examples of generators or motors that were not mentioned in this reading.

From One Current to Another

EVER WONDER?

Have you ever driven past an electric-power generating station and seen huge piles of coal waiting to be burned? Have you ever stood on top of a large dam and wondered why some of the water in the lake was being allowed to run through a spillway? If so, you probably also noticed the great number of power lines coming from these two places.

How are coal and water used to produce electricity? How can you start with water or coal and end up with light in your room or music from your stereo? This investigation will help you discover how one kind of energy can be changed to electricity.

MATERIALS LIST

- Small motor
- Pinwheel
- 3-volt lightbulb with socket
- Strong bonding glue or epoxy (quick-drying variety)
- Plastic bag (1 L)
- Tape (if needed to seal plastic bag)
- Compass
- Safety goggles

STEP-BY-STEP

1 Put on your safety goggles.

2 Slowly move the compass past the motor. Do this several times, in different directions. Record your observations in your logbook.

3 Make a small hole in the bottom of the plastic bag. The hole should be a little larger in diameter than the driveshaft of the motor.

4 Place the motor inside the plastic bag, and push the shaft through the hole.

5 Glue the pinwheel to the end of the shaft that is sticking out of the hole in the bag. Make sure that the blades of the pinwheel face outward, away from the motor. Allow the glue to dry.

6 Screw the lightbulb into the socket. If the socket has screw-type terminals, loosen the screws just enough to allow the end of a wire to fit under the head of a screw.

7 Attach the two wires from the motor to the socket terminals (see Figure 19). If necessary, tighten the screws of the terminals.

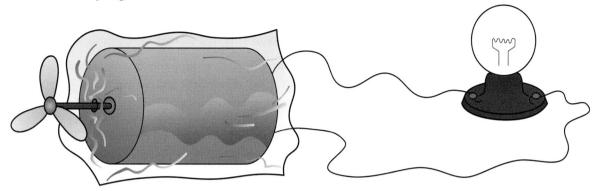

Figure 19: Equipment setup for Investigation 9

8 Pull the plastic bag over the motor and lightbulb. Seal the bag (use tape, if necessary).

9 Have one group member hold the motor carefully and firmly over the sink. Be sure the lightbulb is visible.

10 Have another group member turn on the water faucet so that the running water strikes the blades of the pinwheel, making them turn. Record your observations.

11 Continue holding the pinwheel under the water as another member slowly turns off the water. Record your observations in your logbook.

12 Clean up your work area, and return all materials.

TALK IT OVER

Work with the other members of your group to answer the following questions.

1 When you turned on the water, what kind of energy did the running water have?

2 What kind of energy did the pinwheel and motor shaft have when they were turning?

3 What would you expect to find inside the motor that would account for the fact that the bulb lit up? Explain your idea.

4 Suppose you wanted to generate enough electricity for a whole city. If you wished to create a large-scale version of your experimental equipment, what natural energy sources could you use to turn the shaft of your motor-generator?

SPREAD THE WORD

Work with the others in your group to present the results of your investigation to the class. To help your audience understand what you did, you could make a poster showing the flow of energy from the stream of water to the lightbulb. Label each type of energy, and indicate whether it is transferred, converted to another form, or both. You could also make a simple drawing of the inside of the motor, labeling the different parts and materials. Explain what the various parts of the motor accomplished when you used the motor as a generator.

Find out how the electric company that serves your area produces its power. Also do some research at the library or on the Internet to determine the most important energy sources for producing electric power. List some common things that contain motors or generators, and describe some jobs in which workers would need to understand how motors and generators function.

READ ALL ABOUT IT!

If It Moves, It Has Power

LONG before the discovery of electricity, people used moving water and wind to grind their grain and move their ships. When water or air moves, it has kinetic energy that can be used to move objects such as waterwheels, windmills, and sails. Today billions of people all over the world still rely on water and wind for their power, but they use water, wind, and other sources of energy to produce electricity.

How is electricity produced? How can water moving through the spillway of a dam provide electricity for millions of people?

Power stations all over the world create electricity the same way you did in Investigation 9. They use generators to convert one form of energy, such as the kinetic energy of running water, into electrical energy. The pinwheel and motor that you used is a miniature version of the turbine generators used throughout the world.

A **turbine** is an engine that rotates when a force pushes against its blades. (A windmill is an example of a simple kind of turbine: Wind turns the blades of the windmill's propeller, and these blades turn a shaft.)

The turbine is connected to the shaft of a generator. As the turbine revolves, its kinetic energy is transferred to the generator's shaft. As the shaft of the generator turns, an electric current flows through wire coils around the shaft. Today turbine generators produce nearly all of the world's electricity.

Windmills, such as these at Altamont Pass, California, are actually turbines. Turned by the wind, the propeller blades of each windmill rotate the shaft of a generator. In windy areas, a significant amount of clean electrical energy can be generated by windmills.

POWER FROM THE SUN

Ninety percent of the energy that is used in the United States comes from fossil fuels (coal, oil, and natural gas). These resources are "nonrenewable"—once they are all used up, they cannot be replaced. This means that the world will eventually run out of fossil fuels. How will future generations produce energy?

As fossil fuels become more expensive and get used up, people may turn to solar power to help meet the world's energy needs. The sun emits a tremendous amount of light and heat, but today only 1% of U.S. energy production comes directly from the sun.

Solar energy can produce electricity in two ways. The solar thermal method uses sunlight to boil liquids and produce steam that turns turbines or generators. The Luz Solar Energy Generating System (SEGS) plants near San Bernardino, California, use this approach. California leads the nation in using solar power to generate electricity.

The second method of producing electricity from sunlight involves photovoltaic (PV) cells. These cells are large panels of semiconductors that change sunlight directly into electricity. PV devices are much smaller than solar-thermal plants, but they are much more versatile. They are often used in remote areas where electric lines have not been installed. PV devices are also used to provide energy for emergency workers at sites of natural disasters. Along major highways, PV cells are used to power emergency telephones and signs.

There are many ways to power a turbine generator. When you turn on a light in the United States, you are probably using electric power that is being generated from burning coal or falling water. Some power plants burn coal to boil water. As the water boils, the pressure of hot steam turns a turbine. Here's how the process works: When the coal burns, its chemical potential energy is released as thermal energy (heat). This thermal energy is transferred to the water, which turns to hot steam. The steam produces pressure that turns the turbine.

Other power stations are located at dams or natural waterfalls. When water is forced to fall through a turbine, the kinetic energy of the water is transferred to the blades of the turbine, causing them to rotate. In turn, the kinetic energy of the turbine is transferred to the shaft of a generator. As the shaft turns a magnet surrounded by wire coils, electric current starts to flow through the coils.

MORE POWER TO YOU
In Finland, France, and other countries, nuclear power plants produce much of the

electricity that people use. Nuclear reactors heat water to high temperatures, and the steam is used to drive large turbine generators, just as it is in a coal-fired power plant. Hot steam that runs generators is produced in other ways too. In Iceland and Japan, **geothermal** energy (heat energy from the earth) heats the steam that is used to produce electricity and heat homes. Iceland and Japan are located in active volcanic zones, where the heat inside the earth is close to the surface.

THERE'S A DOWNSIDE

The modern world depends on electricity for many different things: lighting, heating, cooking, air-conditioning, manufacturing. . . . But the various methods used to produce electricity can have negative effects on the environment. Coal produces smoke and gases that pollute the air, water, and land. Nuclear power plants are extremely expensive to build, and they produce radioactive waste that is difficult to dispose of. They also require a great deal of water for cooling. When this water is returned to a river or bay after being used, it is often so warm that it kills the animals and plants in that area.

Damming rivers to produce electric power can also have significant effects on the environment. For example, thousands of acres of land may be submerged by the lake created when a river is dammed. Wind-powered generators do not damage the environment, but there are few places windy enough to produce sufficient power to replace ordinary power plants. For all these reasons, some people have turned to the sun as a source of electrical energy.

The modern world depends on electricity for many different things. . . . But the various methods used to produce electricity can have negative effects on the environment.

THINGS ARE LOOKING UP

Solar energy can be converted directly into electrical energy without using generators. Solar cells made of silicon and other materials convert light energy into electrical energy. Numerous devices, such as wristwatches, cameras, and pocket calculators, use solar cells. NASA, the U.S. Coast Guard, and many telephone companies use solar cells to power certain instruments. And in parts of the world that receive large amounts of sunshine, more and more people are building solar-powered homes.

In most of the world, however, the amount of energy available from sunlight is not great. Extremely large surfaces would be needed to collect as much electricity as people are accustomed to using. It will take a lot more research and effort to produce solar cells that can generate as much electricity as the big power plants you see outside cities all over the world.

ON YOUR OWN

Answer the following questions based on "If It Moves, It Has Power."

1 In the future could batteries be an important power source that might replace waterfalls and coal-burning power plants? Explain.

2 What is the reason a turbine is needed to produce electricity from moving water?

3 How does the production of electric power from sunlight differ from other methods of generating electricity?

SECTION WRAP-UP

Powerful Connections

EVERYONE knows that magnets are useful for sticking notes on refrigerators. But few people know how magnetism affects their lives every day. They depend on the properties of magnets to light their homes, get them to work or school, entertain them, and move them from place to place. In fact, few people realize that they live on a gigantic magnet called Earth.

CLOSE ENOUGH

The planet Earth has its own magnetic north and south poles. These poles are not exactly the same as the geographic poles, but they are close enough to allow you to use a compass to determine directions. The north pole of the compass needle points to the magnetic north pole because the planet's magnetic north pole is actually a pole of "south" magnetism. (Remember, opposite poles attract each other, while similar poles repel.)

A simple compass cannot reveal the shape of the magnetic force field that surrounds Earth or another magnetic object. Although a force field is invisible, you can see the shape of a magnetic field by scattering iron filings around a magnet—the filings will line up according to the lines of force in the magnetic field.

A magnetic field can be used to produce electricity: By changing a magnetic field (moving a magnet) around a coil of wire, you can generate an electric current in the wire. You can reverse this procedure: By passing a current of electricity through a wire, you can produce a magnetic field. These two processes indicate that magnetism and electricity are closely related. They not only share polarity—attractive and repulsive forces—but each process can also produce the other. Basically, electricity and magnetism are two aspects of the same thing: **electromagnetism.**

GET THIS . . .
A magnetic field can be used to produce electricity, and an electric current can be used to produce a magnetic field. Basically, electricity and magnetism are two aspects of the same thing: electromagnetism.

When you turn on your car or play your VCR, you rely on the special relationship between magnetism and electricity. Generators produce electricity by producing an electromagnetic field through the motion of magnets and copper coils. The motion or mechanical force can come from many different sources, including the movement of your hand. But the large amounts of electricity produced for cities and homes require other sources of kinetic energy.

In many parts of the world, falling water or flowing tides turn large turbines that are linked to generators. In places that do not have such water resources, the thermal energy from burning coal or from nuclear reactors is used to heat steam that moves the turbines. In windy places, electricity is generated by using the force of the wind to turn the blades of windmill turbines. Even the hot waters of geysers provide a source of energy for the generation of electricity in a few locations.

In all these cases, one form of energy must be converted by huge generators into electrical energy. And in other cases, as with coal-burning and nuclear power plants, waste products affect the environment in unhealthy ways.

LOOKING TO THE SUN

Today scientists are searching for cleaner, less expensive sources of energy. Much of their attention is focused on the sun. Converting solar energy to electricity does not require huge, complex turbine generators. Solar energy is clean, free, and more

dependable than any other form of energy. But much of the world does not receive enough sunlight to produce as much electricity as people want. Furthermore, the solar-cell panels that convert sunlight to electricity still need a lot of improvement.

Solar energy is clean, free, and more dependable than any other form of energy.

Today's solar panels cannot produce as much electricity as the generators that have been in use for the past hundred years; however, they can produce electricity more efficiently and safely. Until better methods of using solar power are developed, the best way to preserve the world's energy supply and protect the environment may be to build machines and buildings that use less energy and cause less pollution.

This technician is using a reflectometer to measure the surface quality of one of the mirrors that are used to focus the light of the sun onto solar panels.

ON YOUR OWN

Answer the following questions based on "Powerful Connections."

1 How could you show a friend the force field (lines of force) generated by a magnet?

2 If you had to transport a magnet the size of a small car, would you use an airplane or a truck? Give your reasons.

3 Can you think of any machines or appliances in your home that do not require electricity? If so, what is the source of their energy?

CAREER LINKS

Communication Technologies

CABLE-TV INSTALLER

Hooking up TV sets to cable lines requires several different skills but not much formal education: You need to be able to climb utility poles or operate a bucket truck, you must learn how to wire houses and apartment buildings, and you must be able to use electronic devices to measure the strength of the signal in the cable. You also need good interpersonal skills: Dealing with unhappy customers whose cable went out in the middle of their favorite TV show requires a professional level of patience and courtesy. An installer can move up to technician by learning how to adjust amplifiers on the lines and how to control the electronic equipment at the head end (central plant). You can get into the cable field by working under the supervision of an experienced installer. For more information, contact your local cable operator or write:

National Cable Television Association
1724 Massachusetts Avenue, N.W.
Washington, DC 20036

Related occupations: satellite-dish installer, telephone installer, electrician

ELECTRIC BRAINS

PICTURE yourself sitting up in bed with a science book propped against your legs. You should be studying, but you can't seem to get in the mood. Your gaze drifts to the sunny window. Quit daydreaming, you tell yourself. You read a few sentences, but your mind starts wandering again. It wanders back to when you first learned how to read. You see yourself in the first grade. Things you learned years ago are easy now—but they seemed tough then. Science seems tough now. You try to remember what you just read by putting it in your own words. You write a few notes in your logbook. Then you catch yourself doodling. . . .

Each of these activities is controlled by your brain. How does your brain communicate with the rest of your body? How does information from your hands and eyes reach your brain? How do you make sense of what you see, smell, or touch? Do other organisms detect and respond to their experiences the same way you do? What kinds of information must their nervous systems process, and how do they accomplish this? You will explore these questions in this section.

FREEZE FRAME

Now that you have watched the video segment, discuss the following on-screen questions with the other students in your class.

1 How can a person's body generate electricity?

2 What can you tell by measuring a person's brain waves? Can you read the person's thoughts?

Going Buggy

EVER WONDER?

Did you ever turn over a rock or a piece of wood and see a little gray bug scurry away? If so, it was probably a pill bug or a sow bug. They are related to lobsters and shrimp, and they are often called wood lice, roly-polies, or potato bugs. They are completely harmless and almost defenseless. When pill bugs are frightened, they curl up into tight, little balls, but the only defense that sow bugs have is to get away as quickly as possible. Have you ever thought about where bugs such as these live? Do they prefer to live in certain kinds of places? Can such small simple creatures detect different environmental conditions? In this investigation you will learn the answers to these questions.

MATERIALS LIST

- 10 roly-polies in a container
- Assorted liquids, such as vinegar, alcohol, and fruit juices
- 1 petri dish
- Scissors
- 2 pieces of filter paper, cut in half
- Dark paper
- Stopwatch or other timing device

STEP-BY-STEP (PART 1)

1 In your logbook make a data table that is similar to the following sample. (The sample shows only three 30-second intervals. Make your table long enough to hold data that you record every 30 seconds for 10 minutes.)

NUMBER OF ROLY-POLIES ON WET AND DRY FILTER PAPER		
Time (min:sec)	**Wet**	**Dry**
0		
:30		
1:00		
1:30		

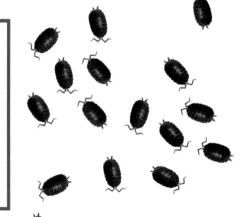

2 Cut your filter paper in half.

3 Moisten one half, but keep the other half dry.

4 Place the two halves on opposite sides of your petri dish. Leave an open area between the pieces of filter paper (see Figure 20).

5 Gently place your 10 bugs in the space between the two halves of filter paper.

6 Observe the behavior of the roly-polies for 10 minutes. Every 30 seconds record in your data table the number of bugs on the wet piece of filter paper and the number of bugs on the dry piece.

7 Add up the figures in the two columns to determine the total number of times bugs were observed on the wet and the dry paper during the 10-minute experimental period. Show the totals at the bottom of the data table.

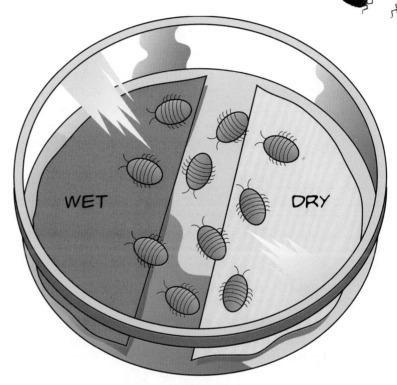

Figure 20: Equipment setup for Investigation 10

STEP-BY-STEP (PART 2)

1 In Part 1 you investigated the ability of roly-polies to detect the difference between moist and dry environments. What other choice of environments could you give them by dividing a petri dish in half? Discuss this with your partner, and decide on the two environments you would like to explore.

2 Discuss which of the two environments your bugs would prefer. Record your prediction in your logbook.

3 When your teacher approves your plan, make a new data table, set up a trial, and record the results as you did in Part 1 of this investigation.

Science L i n k s

TALK IT OVER

Work with your partner to answer the following questions.

1 Do the roly-polies seem to prefer dry or wet filter paper? Explain how your data support your conclusion.

2 How do the bugs detect the difference between wet and dry filter paper?

3 If your bugs showed no preference, does this prove they could not tell the difference between the wet and dry paper? Explain your answer.

4 In Part 2 did the results show that the prediction you made was correct? Explain.

5 How could the roly-polies' behavior that you observed help them to survive?

6 Based on what you have learned in this investigation, what evidence do you have that roly-polies can make choices that help them survive?

SPREAD THE WORD

Work with your partner to plan a presentation of your results and conclusions to the class. You could start by explaining what you learned about the roly-polies' responses to different environments. You might want to display your data table on a transparency or poster. Suggest a reason why roly-polies behave as they do. Tell how your findings can be applied in the real world. For example, explain how someone could get rid of a large number of roly-polies in the basement without using bug sprays, which might be dangerous for people to inhale.

Who else might need to know how animals detect and respond to differences in their environments? Think of some other ways that people can use knowledge of this animal behavior at work or at home, and share your ideas with the class.

READ ALL ABOUT IT!

This Is Getting on My Nerves

RESPONDING to environmental changes is a basic process of life. Every organism—including you—must react to its own environment and to changes that occur there. The reaction of an organism to a change is called a **response**. The environmental change that causes the organism to respond is a **stimulus**. The roly-polies in Investigation 10 responded to wet and dry filter paper. The presence or absence of moisture was the stimulus to which they responded.

How did the roly-polies know one side of the petri dish was different from the other? Animals have specialized cells that allow them to detect temperature, light, sound, and other environmental conditions. These cells are important to an animal's survival. In humans and other vertebrates (animals with backbones), the stimulus information that these cells receive is sent by nerves to the brain or spinal cord. After the information is processed there, a response message is sent through nerves to a muscle or gland.

Much the same thing happens with a roly-poly, even though its nervous system is a lot simpler than a human's.

NETWORK OF NERVES

The nervous system of humans and other vertebrates can be divided into two major parts: the **central nervous system**, which consists of the brain and spinal cord, and the **peripheral nervous system**, which consists of nerves that connect the central nervous system to other parts of the body (see Figure 21).

The **spinal cord** carries information from the brain to the body nerves or from the body nerves to the brain. Persons with severe spinal injuries are often paralyzed below the point of the injury. Paralysis occurs because information can no longer be transferred between different parts of the nervous system.

The average human brain has billions of cells and weighs about 1,500 g. The brain is soft and jellylike. A blow to the head or severe shaking can cause brain damage. For protection, the brain is surrounded by a series of membranes and the skull.

The brain has three major parts: cerebrum, cerebellum, and brain stem (see Figure 22). Each part has a different function.

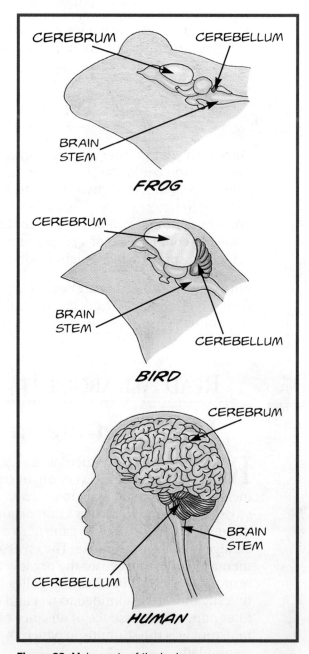

Figure 22: Major parts of the brain

Figure 21: The human nervous system

The **cerebrum** controls your thoughts, reasoning, personality, and muscular movements, including responses to information from your five senses (seeing, hearing, smelling, tasting, feeling). The cerebrum also stores the messages from your sensory organs so that they can be recalled later. These messages—for example, the aroma of freshly baked bread, the way to get home, your best friend's phone number, or your own name—are the contents of your memory. The cerebrum is the largest part of the brain (about 85% of its weight).

The **cerebellum** is located at the rear of the brain. It controls balance, posture, and coordination. The **brain stem** is a stalklike mass at the upper end of the spinal cord. It sorts information in such a way that some stimuli reach your conscious attention while others do not. This sorting explains why you are not aware of the shoes on your feet all the time but you will feel a tiny bug crawling up your leg. The brain stem also controls involuntary functions, such as breathing and digestion.

You can learn a great deal about the behavior of animals by examining their brains. For example, while the cerebellum is well-developed in humans, it is even more developed in birds (see Figure 22). The reason is that birds have adapted to perform complicated acts of balance. They can fly

SPLIT PERSONALITY

If your cerebrum gets damaged, you could end up with a new personality. That's what happened to Phineas Gage, a 25-year-old railroad foreman, in 1884. Gage was laying track on the Burlington Railroad in Vermont when a blasting accident sent an iron rod through his face and brain and on into the sky.

The rod, which was 10 cm long and 3 cm in diameter, stunned Gage for a moment, but he immediately regained full consciousness. He was able to talk and to walk. In fact, he went on to live another 20 years. But something changed. Before the accident, Gage had been a responsible, intelligent man. After the accident, he was still strong and able to work, but his personality was different and he could not keep a job. His friends said he was no longer Phineas Gage.

Gage's skull and the iron rod have been preserved at Harvard University. Using MRI (Magnetic Resonance Imaging), X rays, and three-dimensional reconstruction, scientists have been able to determine exactly what portion of Gage's cerebrum was destroyed. It was the region that controls the ability to make decisions and control emotions.

Researchers have learned a great deal about the human brain by studying individuals such as Phineas Gage. Today if someone has a stroke or head injury, doctors can predict how that person's life will be affected. Moreover, in cases where no external injury occurs, a change in personality may indicate the existence of brain damage.

through the air very fast and suddenly land on a thin branch or wire without falling off.

An animal's nervous system is a lot like a computer system. Both perform many complex tasks. Both use input and output devices. The body uses sensory organs for input, while a computer uses a keyboard, mouse, scanner, and other devices. In a computer, input information is translated into code and sent along wires to a central processing unit. The computer responds by displaying data or printing a document.

Monitors and printers are output devices. Similarly the central nervous system processes sensory data and sends information along nerves to the muscles and glands.

In computers, information is transmitted from input to output devices using electricity that travels through wires. In the next set of investigations, you will learn how information about the environment is transmitted into an animal's cells and then through its nervous system so that it can respond appropriately to a stimulus.

ON YOUR OWN

Respond to the following items based on "This Is Getting on My Nerves."

1 You are walking home from school. Describe a common stimulus you might encounter and the response you would make to it.

2 Different regions of an animal's brain deal with the senses of sight and smell. Moles spend their entire lives underground unless something disturbs them. Based on what you have learned, predict how these regions in a mole's brain compare (in level of development) with the corresponding regions in a human brain. Explain your answer.

3 The polio virus attacks and destroys nerve cells connected to muscles. Even though the muscle cells themselves are not damaged by the virus, a person with polio is often paralyzed. Is the polio victim's main problem receiving a stimulus, transmitting the information, or responding to the information? Explain.

INVESTIGATION 11

The Nose Knows

EVER WONDER?

Have you ever sat in a classroom where you could smell food cooking in the cafeteria far away? Have you ever wondered how the smell of food travels so far from where the food is being prepared? How does your nose detect those smells? How does your nose know it is smelling food, and how does it pass the message to your brain? In the following demonstrations, you will observe how some substances can move through water and enter a sealed container. This will help you understand how food odors move through the air and penetrate the sensory cells in your nose.

In or Out?

EVER WONDER?

Does an ocean fish taste saltier than a freshwater fish? How is an animal affected by living in salt water? Does it adjust by becoming as salty as the water? Or can living things control what enters and leaves their bodies so that their insides stay the same, no matter what changes outside them? In this investigation you will discover how living cells control what passes through their membranes.

MATERIALS LIST

- Compound light microscope
- Lens paper
- 2 microscope slides
- 2 coverslips
- Wax pencil
- Beaker of uncooked yeast culture, with Congo red stain added
- Beaker of cooked yeast culture, with Congo red stain added
- 2 dropper pipets (medicine droppers)
- Sheet of unlined paper
- Pencil
- Red marker

STEP-BY-STEP

1 Use a wax pencil to label two microscope slides: Put "Live" on one slide and "Heat-Killed" on the other.

2 Use a pipet to put a drop of live yeast culture in the center of the "Live" slide. Place a coverslip over the drop.

3 Locate the live yeast under low magnification of your microscope. Use your logbook to describe what you see.

4 Next, locate the live yeast under high magnification. Again use your logbook to describe what you see.

5 Using a pencil, draw several of these yeast cells. Use a red marker to indicate any red areas that you observe. Label the cells, and indicate the magnification.

6 Set aside this slide. Do not clean it off. You may need to observe it again.

7 Use the other pipet to place a drop of heat-killed yeast culture on the "Heat-Killed" slide. Place a coverslip over the drop.

8 Locate the yeast under low magnification of your microscope. In your logbook describe what you see.

9 Locate the heat-killed yeast under high magnification. Record what you see.

10 Using a pencil, draw several of these yeast cells. Use the red marker to indicate any red areas you observe. Label the cells, and indicate the magnification.

TALK IT OVER

Work with your partner to answer the following questions.

1 Which one of the two slides contains mostly red yeast cells?

2 Look at the other slide. What is the reason that a few cells on it are red while the others have remained unstained?

3 How might the cells in one yeast culture be able to prevent the Congo red stain from entering, while the cells in the other culture could not do so? (Hint: Remember that cell membranes are barriers and that they have not been damaged in either culture.)

CAREER LINKS

Health & Human Services

World Bank

PSYCHOLOGIST

Psychologists and psychiatrists analyze human behavior by examining how the mind works. They must understand how chemicals produce electricity in the brain, how information flows through the nervous system, and how other complex processes work. To become a psychiatrist, you must obtain an M.D. (doctor of medicine) degree and then serve a two- to six-year residency period to gain experience. A psychiatrist may choose to treat mentally ill patients either in a private practice or on the staff of an institution. The science of psychology focuses on the mind and behavior. To become a psychologist, you must obtain a master's degree in clinical psychology. Some psychologists enter private practice or work on the staff of a school, hospital, or company. Others study the behavior of animals to learn about human mental processes. For more information, write:

American Psychological Association
Education Directorate
750 1st Street, N.E.
Washington, DC 20002
http://www.apa.org/ed/ed.html

Related occupations: neurological surgeon, pharmacologist, medical examiner, clinical technician, mental-health counselor

Science L i n k s

SPREAD THE WORD

Help other students learn what you have discovered in this investigation. Work with your partner to plan a presentation of your results and conclusions.

Make a poster or overhead transparency to illustrate what happened to allow the Congo red to enter yeast cells in one culture but not in the other. Use labels and arrows to make your ideas clear to the rest of the class. Here is another way to help your audience understand what you learned: Draw an analogy (show a similarity) between a cell membrane and some nonliving barrier. Think of such a barrier that has stopped working but is not broken—it simply cannot function, and this prevents people or objects from passing through it. Explain what caused the barrier to stop working. Use this idea to produce a model of how a cell membrane works.

Explain why different kinds of workers may need to understand how body cells control what passes across their membranes.

GET THIS . . .

Diffusion is a process in which substances that are dissolved in gases or liquids tend to move from areas where they are highly concentrated to areas where they are less concentrated.

READ ALL ABOUT IT!

Active or Passive?

SUBSTANCES that are soluble (able to dissolve) in gases and liquids tend to move outward from areas where they are highly concentrated to areas where they are less concentrated. This process is called **diffusion**. It occurs because all molecules, even those in solids, are in constant motion.

Diffusion occurs because all molecules, even those in solids, are in constant motion.

When you make lemonade from scratch, you mix lemon juice, water, and sugar; then you stir the ingredients. Why do you stir them? To mix the sugar and the liquids. At first the sugar molecules that have dissolved in the water are mostly near the bottom, around the undissolved sugar. At the edge

of this region, some of the sugar molecules gradually move into the surrounding water. At the same time, some of the water molecules wander in among the sugar molecules. If you did not stir, the random motion and collisions of water and sugar molecules would eventually cause them to mix evenly, but this would take an awfully long time.

SAVE YOUR ENERGY

Some substances, such as salt and water, can diffuse even through the tiny pores in certain membranes, such as dialysis tubing, while other substances, such as starch, are unable to do so. A membrane that allows only some substances to pass through it is described as **selectively permeable**. Your kidneys, for example, contain selectively permeable membranes that allow wastes and excess salt to pass out of your bloodstream; but these membranes do not allow important proteins to escape. This is one way that your kidneys help keep you healthy.

In Investigation 12 you saw that other living things, such as yeast cells, can also control the diffusion of materials in and out of their cells. A fish too can keep a healthy salt concentration in its cells whether it lives in salt water or fresh water. The cells of fish and other living things are surrounded by a selectively permeable membrane that restricts the flow of salt in and out of the cells.

JUST PASSING THROUGH

Some other substances pass through cell membranes more easily: When food substances are more concentrated outside the cells than inside, they can diffuse in through the cell membranes without requiring the cells to use any of their own energy to absorb the food. In the same way, waste substances that are more concentrated inside cells than outside can diffuse outward.

Cell membranes also contain special proteins that act as "channels," allowing specific substances to pass in or out of cells more easily than they would otherwise (see Figure 23). Because the substances are automatically transported through the membrane, with no cellular action, this process is called **passive transport**. ("Passive" is the opposite of "active.") Water nearly always passes through membranes by passive transport.

TAKING ACTION

Diffusion is too slow to explain some of the things that cells do. For example, it takes your brain less than a second to send a message to the muscles in your hands to start moving. This is much faster than any chemical signal could diffuse through your body.

In Investigation 12 you saw that living cells can keep out foreign substances, such as Congo red stain, but dead cells cannot. Living cells can use their own energy to operate tiny "pumps"—special proteins in their membranes that can move specific substances in or out of the cells. This process is called **active transport** (see Figure 24). The red dye diffused into both living and dead yeast cells, but the living cells were able to pump it out faster than it diffused inward. The living cells used active transport to push the dye out, even though it was more concentrated on the outside. Active transport can move substances in or out of cells against the flow of diffusion. This

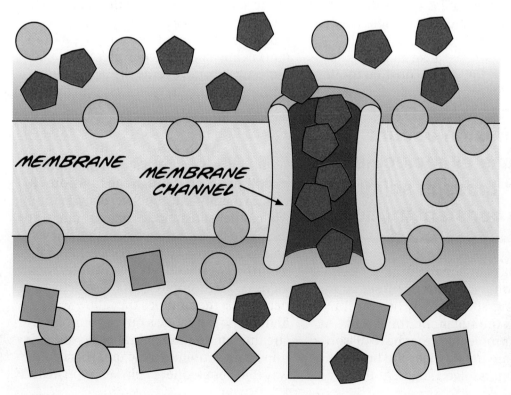

MEMBRANE

MEMBRANE CHANNEL

Figure 23: Passive transport through a selectively permeable membrane
Note: Some substances (yellow circles) diffuse easily through cell membranes, while others (green squares) do not. Special proteins that act as "channels" permit some substances (red pentagons) that do not pass easily through cell membranes to enter or leave cells.

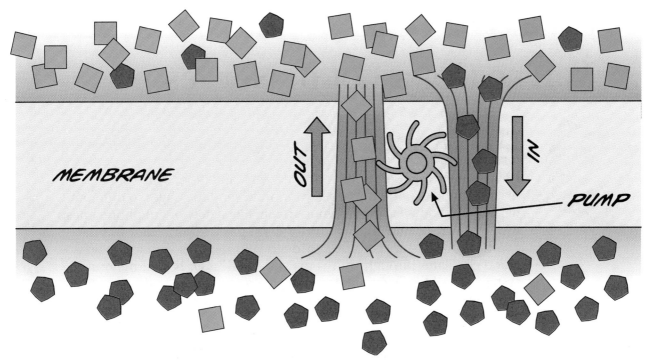

Figure 24: Active transport through a selectively permeable membrane
Note: A cell can use its own energy to operate a "pump"—a special protein in the cell membrane—to transport substances in or out of the cell. In this example, sodium ions (green squares) are carried out and potassium ions (red pentagons) are carried in.

process enables every cell in your body to absorb nutrients from your bloodstream and to pump out wastes that your bloodstream carries off. Plants use the same process to absorb nutrients from the soil. All living things depend on active transport.

The concept of active transport does not apply only to nutrients and wastes. It also involves nerve cells. As you will learn in the next investigation, active transport is critical to the transfer of stimulus and response messages throughout your nervous system.

ON YOUR OWN

Answer the following questions based on "Active or Passive?"

1 When you breathe, oxygen passes—by diffusion—from the air in your lungs to your bloodstream. Is the concentration of oxygen greater in your blood or in the air? Explain.

2 Potassium is an important ion used by plant and animal cells. Plant root cells constantly absorb it from the surrounding soil. Potassium's concentration within a plant root cell is typically about 10 times greater than the surrounding soil. By what mechanism do root cells take in potassium? Explain your answer.

3 Sodium is an ion that is essential to the proper functioning of nerve cells. The concentration of sodium ions is much lower inside a nerve cell than in the surrounding body fluids. Would you expect sodium ions to move into or out of a nerve cell? What process could help maintain such a difference in sodium concentration between the inside and outside of a nerve cell? Explain.

You've Got a Lot of Nerves

EVER WONDER?

How does information from your eyes, ears, and other sense organs reach your brain? And how does your brain send messages to different parts of the body? Is your nervous system like a network of phone lines, with tiny wires connecting all the different parts of your body to one another? Or do nerve cells flow through your nervous system the way blood circulates through your veins and arteries? Or is your nervous system more like the circuit boards inside a computer? In this investigation you will watch a video segment that will help you discover exactly how your nervous system works.

The nervous system of a small creature such as this sea slug can help you understand how your own nervous system works.

READ ALL ABOUT IT!

How Impulsive Are You?

WHEN a dog smells something good to eat in the kitchen, it begins to drool. How do the salivary glands in the dog's mouth get the message to start drooling? Suppose you accidentally touch a hot burner on a stove. What makes your hand pull away before you even think about getting burned?

The messages about drooling or pulling away your hand are transmitted by special cells called **neurons**. Like other cells in the body, neurons have a cell membrane, cytoplasm, and organelles, including a nucleus.

But neurons have a different shape: They are long and thin, with branches on one end and a threadlike extension on the other (see Figure 25).

PASS IT ON

The branches, which are called **dendrites**, receive information from the five senses (sight, smell, hearing, touch, and taste) or from other neurons, and they relay the information to the rest of the cell. The information is then passed on to other cells by the **axon**, the threadlike structure at the other end of the **cell body**, which is the main part of the cell, containing the nucleus. This is how messages travel from the senses to the central nervous system and from the central nervous system to muscles and glands.

When a neuron is not receiving messages, it uses active transport to pump out positively charged sodium ions (Na+) through its cell membrane. As more sodium gets pushed out, a positive charge builds up outside the cell. The inside of the cell loses positive charges and becomes negatively charged.

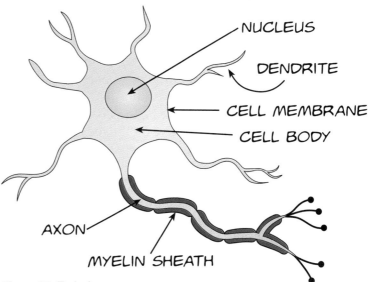

This imbalance between the outside charge and the inside charge is a voltage called the **resting potential**. Sodium can sometimes diffuse back into the cell through special sodium channels in the membrane, but at this time the channels are closed. With the sodium pump working in only one direction (sending positive ions out), no current can flow. The neuron's cell membrane is now like a disconnected battery.

Figure 25: Typical neuron

FEELING MANIC? DEPRESSED? CHECK YOUR IONS

A "manic-depressive" person has wild mood swings—excited and hyper sometimes, sad and miserable other times. This condition, which is also called "bipolar affective disorder," is a serious psychological problem.

In the 1940s, John Cade, an Australian psychiatrist. began to suspect that toxins (poisons) in the blood caused this problem. To test his theory, he experimented on guinea pigs to examine the effects of different components of urine, which contains toxins from blood. But he had trouble injecting one toxin, uric acid, because it did not dissolve in water. He discovered that the most soluble form of uric acid is a lithium compound. In further tests, one of the lithium compounds that he injected had a calming effect on the guinea pigs. This led him to focus on the effect of lithium on the human nervous system.

Scientists now know that manic-depressive people have difficulty maintaining a high-enough ion imbalance across the membranes of neurons. The imbalance causes their neurons to be overstimulated. Lithium ions (Li+) help restore the proper amounts of positive charge on the outside of the neurons and negative charge on the inside. This raises the resting potential of neurons to its normal level and reduces the level of stimulation.

Lithium and other drugs that alter the activity level of neurons are called psychoactive drugs. Unlike lithium, some psychoactive drugs have the opposite effect on the nervous system: They overstimulate neurons. For example, cocaine causes neurons to produce many extra action potentials every time they are stimulated. Each new action potential restarts the process

Such overstimulation is dangerous because it prevents the brain from processing the stimulus information properly. Eventually it can cause damage to the entire nervous system, especially the brain.

An incoming message "connects" the "battery": The message turns on the current through part of the membrane in a dendrite. This electrical impulse opens the sodium channels in the membrane that covers the dendrite, and sodium ions flood in, reversing the voltage (see Figure 26). The dendrite becomes positive on the inside and negative on the outside.

IMPULSE POWER

When one part of the membrane changes voltage, it affects the neighboring parts. Nearby sodium channels open, reversing the charge in the next part of the membrane. Each portion of the cell membrane passes the voltage pulse to the next. The pulse passes all the way to the tip of the axon. This traveling electrical message is called an **action potential** or **nerve impulse**. After an action potential passes, the sodium

channels close and the sodium pumps restore the resting potential.

When the electrical message reaches the end of a neuron's axon, it must cross a gap called a **synapse**. A special chemical passes

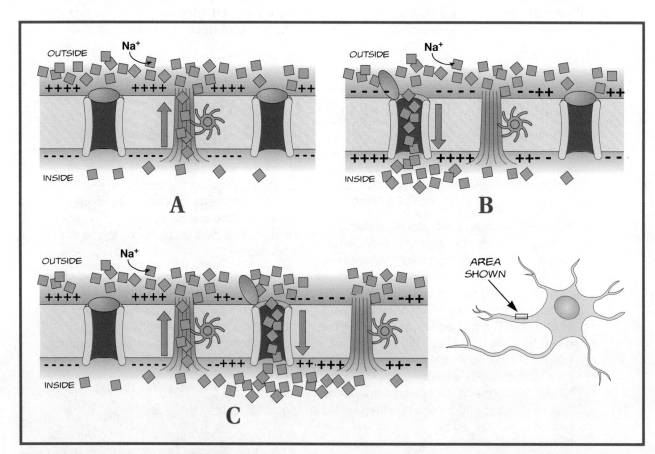

Figure 26: Movement of an action potential

Note: (A) shows part of the cell membrane at rest—sodium channels (purple) are closed, and a membrane pump (represented here by the light-blue wheel) carries sodium ions out of the cell, making the outside positive and the inside negative. An action potential arrives from the left in (B)—the sodium pump stops, the left channel in the diagram opens, and sodium floods in, reversing the membrane voltage. In (C) the voltage change causes neighboring channels to open and pumps to stop, passing the impulse along.

across the synapse, activating the dendrites of the next neuron. Messages keep getting transmitted until they reach the appropriate cells. If the destination is a salivary gland cell in a dog's mouth, the action potentials stimulate the gland and the dog begins to drool. Another message might go to the leg muscles, telling them to contract so that the dog can move closer to the food it smells.

ALL THE SAME

Lots of neurons that are bundled together make up a **nerve**. Nerves transmit many kinds of messages. A neuron may send a signal to the brain that your hand is touching a dangerously hot stove—or a pleasantly warm bath.

How do the neurons signal the difference between strong and mild messages? All action potentials are identical; therefore, stronger messages do not produce larger membrane voltages. The strength of the message is encoded in the number of action potentials that are sent per second—the more impulses transmitted, the stronger the response. Some messages are as strong as 100 impulses per second.

But what if neurons in the same bundle are sending different messages? How do the neurons know which messages to accept and which ones to ignore? Like insulation

THE SPINE IS QUICKER THAN THE BRAIN

If you touch a hot iron, you pull your finger away—and then you feel the pain. Why is there a delayed reaction?

The distance from a body nerve to the brain is greater than the distance from a body nerve to the spinal cord. As a result, it often takes longer for a message to reach your brain than your spinal cord. To minimize damage to body tissues, the spinal cord directs reflex actions, which require quick responses, such as getting your finger off the iron. The message from your finger reaches your brain a split second later; therefore, you don't feel the pain until after you yank your finger away. If your nervous system did not respond reflexively, your finger would get a more severe burn.

You can test your own reflexes at home. To do so, you will need some pictures that make you happy, other pictures that make you sad or upset, and a metric ruler. You will also need another person to help you conduct the test.

Start by facing the other person, who should use the ruler to observe and measure the size of your pupils. Next, look at the pictures in random order. As you examine each one, tell your partner if the picture shows something that is pleasant or unpleasant. As you look at each picture, your partner should observe the size of your pupils and record any changes in size. After you examine at least four or five pictures, look at the data your partner has recorded. How did the size of your pupils change as you looked at the various pictures?

around electrical wires, axons are covered with a fatty material called **myelin**. This keeps the messages from getting mixed up and going to the wrong cells. Sometimes messages do get confused, but usually the electrochemical communication system in your body is extremely reliable.

ON YOUR OWN

Respond to the following items based on "How Impulsive Are You?"

1 How are a nerve and a section of electrical cable alike? How are they different?

2 Normally a natural pacemaker region of the heart signals the heart to beat at regular intervals. People with certain kinds of heart problems have electronic pacemakers, which take over this job. The artificial pacemaker sends out weak electrical impulses. Describe at least two things that the natural and artificial pacemakers must have in common to do their jobs.

3 The puffer fish contains a deadly chemical, tetrodotoxin, in its liver and ovaries. The chemical keeps sodium ions from moving across the membranes of neurons. How does tetrodotoxin bring about the death of an animal that is unfortunate enough to eat a puffer fish?

4 Why would a diet that is low in potassium be hazardous to your health?

5 If someone softly brushes the sole of your foot with a feather, you do not respond. But if someone applies enough pressure with the feather to tickle your foot, you *do* respond. Use your knowledge of how nerve impulses work to explain both situations.

6 Would you expect to find mainly the dendrites or mainly the axons of neurons in your eyes and nose? Give your reasons.

SECTION WRAP-UP

From One Nerve to Another

PICTURE yourself walking down the street after school. As you walk along, you're thinking about what happened in your classes today or what you want to do tonight. You're *not* thinking about moving your legs and feet with each step. Your legs are moving because neurons in several parts of your brain are firing off action potentials toward the cells that control the muscles in your legs. This process occurs in a regular, almost automatic rhythm. It does not involve much of the surface layer of your cerebrum, where conscious, deliberate movements begin.

As you approach a row of shops, molecules that have diffused from buildings and through the air begin to reach your nose. These molecules stimulate neurons in your nose to begin sending action potentials to the part of your cerebrum that is responsible for your sense of smell. One smell gets even stronger as you pass the shops—the action potentials are more frequent, with dozens of them reaching your brain every second.

What's that smell? As your cerebrum tries to sort out the various sensations it is receiving,

it sends a signal to your neck muscles to turn toward the shop windows. Your cerebellum coordinates the action potentials to your neck and leg muscles so that you can turn your head smoothly and keep walking at the same time.

As you approach a row of shops, molecules that have diffused from buildings and through the air begin to reach your nose. . . . What's that smell?

Now your eyes get involved. Light stimulates cells in your eyes to send action potentials to your brain. Again your cerebrum is in charge, assembling all the signals from thousands of neurons into an organized impression of what you see: a window full of pizza! It's a new pizza place. Now neurons that connect your cerebrum to the hunger center in your brain stem pass the message that food has been spotted.

STIMULATING THE NEURONS

As one neuron stimulates another, sodium channels open in the membranes that cover their dendrites. Positive sodium ions rush in, reversing the voltage across a small patch of membrane in each cell. In neighboring parts of the membrane, active sodium transport stops and more sodium channels open, passing along the voltage pulse. The dendrite membranes recover, and the process is repeated again and again, sending hundreds of pulses down axons into your brain stem, where the dendrites of neurons in your hunger center are located.

The message travels quickly down the myelin-insulated axons. At the tips of the axons of these cells, a chemical transmitter is released. It passes across a small gap from each axon to a brain-stem cell's dendrite, provoking a new action potential in the dendrites. The brain-stem neurons pass the signal along their axons to glands in your mouth and stomach. Suddenly you find that your mouth is watering and you feel hungry. (That's funny. You didn't feel hungry a minute ago.) You stop and stare at the window as you decide what to do.

PIZZA TIME

Nerves carry instructions from your cerebrum to muscles in your fingers, telling them to contract. Your fingers then wrap around objects in your pocket. Touch- and temperature-sensing neurons in your fingertips report back that they are in contact with hard, flat, cool objects: money. It's time to put that money to work. Time for some pizza!

You deserve it because, with all the thinking you did in school today, you must have used up a lot of energy actively transporting sodium out of your neurons. You'd better eat something before you fade away.

ON YOUR OWN

Answer the following questions based on "From One Nerve to Another."

1 Before filling a tooth, dentists inject an anesthetic near the nerves that lead into your mouth. What are some possible ways in which the anesthetic could block the sensation of pain from reaching your brain?

2 One treatment for manic-depressive disorders is electroconvulsive therapy. Doctors transmit electric charges through a patient's brain to help restore normal neural function. What might this treatment do to the neural tissues to improve a person's mental state?

3 Some nerves are more easily stimulated than others. Would a more sensitive neuron have a voltage across its membrane that is more positive on the outside or the inside?

MODULE WRAP-UP

Current Thoughts—
A Study of Electricity and Magnetism

WHAT would it be like to ride a space shuttle to the International Space Station and live there for a few months? Electricity is probably not the first thing on your mind as you imagine such a trip, but electricity would be involved every step of the way.

Sitting in your seat, as you wait to blast off into the sky, you look out the window.

As you check for storm clouds, light falls on the back of your eye, stimulating special sensory cells that are in contact with the neurons that make up your optic nerve, connecting your eyes to your brain. The light is just the stimulus to provoke sodium channels in these cells to open, starting a series of action potentials that travel along axons to your brain, where other neurons will sort and assemble the information into a picture of the window and sky. . . .

You see nothing but clear blue sky. That's good. Last night the flight controllers said that the mission might have to be postponed because of a possibility of thunderstorms. If the shuttle were launched while thunderclouds were overhead, the spacecraft could be struck by lightning while it rose through the atmosphere. As it stands on the launch pad, the shuttle is protected by a lightning rod located above the top of the craft.

Because the lightning rod is the highest nearby point that is connected to the ground, it draws lightning away from the shuttle. If lightning struck the shuttle, a tremendous amount of electrical current would probably pass through its delicate electronic circuits and destroy them. But that's not the worst thing that could happen—you don't even want to think about what all those extra electrons would do around the liquid oxygen tanks.

Luckily the thunderclouds are still too far away to threaten your mission. The countdown is continuing, and it's almost time to blast off. The cables that supplied the electric power to the shuttle from outside are pulled away, and your batteries take over. Inside the batteries, a slow reaction involving oxidation and re-action begins. This reaction generates a flow of current through all the circuits that are operating at this time. There are many such circuits, and every one of them has two or three backup systems wired in parallel.

It's time for you to start entering some computer commands to put those circuits to work.

You've practiced this so many times that you hardly have to think about it. And you certainly don't have time to think about how electricity works in your own "circuits." If you did have the time, you could describe this sequence of events:

The neurons in your cerebrum are firing off action potentials to other neurons, which connect them to the muscles in your fingers. The voltage across the membranes in these nerves approaches zero and reverses direction, from positive on the outside to positive on the inside. Now membrane channels open up and sodium ions rush into the nerve cells. Soon the brief reversal of voltage is over, and the ion pumps in the nerve-cell membrane begin to remove the excess sodium. The voltage pulses reach the nerve endings in each muscle in your hand and arms, stimulating them to contract in a coordinated sequence to type the codes you have memorized.

DIGITAL MESSAGES

The computer processes the codes you key into it. The voltage supplied to its disk drive causes a current to flow through the motor's coils, creating a magnetic field that repels the field of the motor's permanent magnets. The two magnetic fields push each other apart, spinning the motor around and letting the computer "read" each part of the disk that it needs to read. Tiny magnetized zones on the disk are another kind of code. They produce voltages in the computer that will be read as digital messages.

The crew waiting for you on the space station is also busy. One crew member is replacing filters in a water-recycling system that uses an artificial membrane as one step in water purification. Water molecules pass easily through the membrane, but many of the impurities in wastewater do not. Batteries store energy to run the space station's equipment. To avoid wasting voltage, the electrical circuits are built of wire that has low resistance. But for safety's sake, the insulation around the electrical equipment is made of a special thick and strong plastic with very low conductivity. It would take much more voltage to break through this coating than is ever likely to occur in these circuits.

The countdown continues: 10, 9, 8, 7. . . . Soon you will be in orbit and you can start your experiments . . . that is, once you have gotten used to living in outer space.

GET THIS . . .

The nervous system of humans and other vertebrates consists of the central nervous system (the brain and spinal cord) and the peripheral nervous system (nerves that connect the central nervous system to other parts of the body).

ON YOUR OWN

Answer the following questions based on the Module Wrap-up.

1 What are some of the differences between the way a computer and a nerve cell use pulsed digital codes to send information?

2 Would there be any advantage to putting a lightning rod on the shuttle? Explain.

3 Some compasses consist of a spherical magnet that floats in a clear glass or plastic ball filled with water or clear oil. This allows the magnet to rotate in three dimensions. If you had such a compass on board the space shuttle, how would it behave as you rode into space?

How to Use Your Logbook

Aʟʟ through *Science Links* you will use a logbook to keep records of your work. A logbook is an important tool in scientific investigation. It provides a place to take notes, collect data, enter observations and conclusions, and jot down questions and ideas. Most scientists keep a log like this one.

In science it is essential to keep accurate records. The information that you collect is valuable—you must work to get it! So write down your ideas before you forget them.

Your logbook will also help you share your ideas with other students. In most of your investigations, you will work as a member of a group. In any situation where people must work together, whether it's flying a jetliner or leading cheers at a basketball game, teamwork is critical. One of the most important aspects of teamwork is communication. No team can succeed unless its members communicate effectively with one another.

Good Writing Is Clear and Simple

Effective communication means writing and speaking in ways that other people will understand. Your logbook can help you develop a good writing style. Whenever you make an entry, try to express your thoughts as clearly and simply as possible. When you finish writing, step back and look at the words as though you are reading them for the first time. If someone else had made this entry, would you be able to understand it? Is the writing clear? Does it cover all the points it was supposed to? You know what you meant to say, but did you succeed in saying it? If you have any doubts, go back to work on the entry.

Writing makes you more aware of your thinking process. This is useful in science because sometimes you don't even realize that you do not understand a concept until you try to express it. Communicating scientific ideas through writing and discussion helps you understand what you are doing. And in *Science Links* the emphasis is on doing science.

Your logbook gives you an opportunity to show your teacher what you have learned. It will reveal how you and the other members of your group are collaborating. The notes you take during presentations by other groups will show if you are receiving useful information from them.

Organizing Your Logbook

Your logbook should be organized chronologically. Every time you make a new entry, put the date in the upper left-hand corner of the page. Next, in the upper right-hand corner, write a few words that tell what the entry is about. Then write the entry itself. (A sample entry appears on the next page.)

Various types of entries are possible. Here are some of them:

- notes based on what occurs during procedures (**Step-by-Step**)
- summaries of group or class discussions (**Talk It Over**)
- outlines for presentations by your group (**Spread the Word**)
- notes and questions about presentations by other groups
- data collected through research
- ideas for projects or reports
- personal views concerning *Science Links* activities

Use your logbook regularly. It will help you keep track of and understand the science you are doing in *Science Links*.

September 30, 1998

Module 2, Investigation 4
Calculations and Observations

Step-by-Step

Step 4
baking soda & paper	5.46 g
paper	−3.46
baking soda	2.00 g

Step 9
| beaker & contents | 123.76 g |
Step 12
| beaker & contents after reaction | −122.31 |
| weight lost | 1.45 g |

After Kim poured the vinegar in the beaker, it foamed up. Giselle said it smelled sour.

Step 14
baking soda & paper	4.83 g
paper	−2.83
baking soda	2.00 g

Step 21
| bottle & contents | 90.50 g |
Step 23
| beaker & contents after reaction | −90.30 |
| weight lost | 0.20 g |

After I poured the vinegar out, it foamed up.

Talk It Over

#1–4. Everybody agreed that the beaker lost more weight than the bottle. Kim said this was because something turned into a gas and it went out of the beaker but couldn't get out of the bottle.

Module Glossary

action potential—a brief voltage pulse that travels over a neuron's membrane to the tip of its axon (74)

active transport—the use of energy by a living cell to move a substance across a membrane against the direction that it would diffuse by itself (70)

ampere (amp)—a unit of current, equal to one coulomb of charge passing a point in a circuit per second (11)

axis—an imaginary line around which something turns (46)

axon—a long extension of a nerve cell that carries action potentials to other cells (72)

bit—a single 0 or 1 of digital information (39)

brain stem—the lowest part of the brain; the brain stem connects the brain to the spinal cord (65)

cell body—the largest part of a nerve cell, containing the nucleus and located between the dendrites and the axon (73)

central nervous system—the part of the nervous system consisting of the brain and spinal cord (64)

cerebellum—the brain part controlling balance and coordination of movement (65)

cerebrum—the part of the brain responsible for perception, thought, and control of muscle movement (64)

circuit—a pathway for electric current that permits it to make a round-trip (11)

circuit breaker—an automatic switch that shuts off a circuit if the current becomes large enough to cause damage (13)

conductivity—the ability to carry an electric current (26)

coulomb—a unit of charge equal to the charge of 6.24 billion billion electrons or protons (11)

current electricity—the movement of a stream of charges through a wire or other object; the size of an electrical current is measured in amperes (5)

dendrite—a neuron extension that can be stimulated by another neuron (72)

diffusion—the slow spread of dissolved substances through a liquid or gas, caused by the random movement of molecules (69)

digital code—a system of 0s and 1s or any other pair of symbols, such as current "on" and "off," used to represent information (39)

electromagnetism—electricity and magnetism, understood as two parts of the same phenomenon (57)

electromotive series—a list of substances (usually metals) arranged in order of how easily they give up electrons (36)

electron—the atomic particle with the smallest unit of negative electrical charge (5)

electroplating—the use of electricity to deposit a layer of metal on a surface (35)

fuse—a device inserted in a circuit and meant to burn or melt if the current becomes great enough to cause damage to other parts of the circuit (12)

Galvanic effect—the tendency of current to flow between two metals when they are placed in contact with each other (35)

generator—a device used to produce electrical power by rotating a magnet inside a wire coil or by rotating a coil inside a magnet (51)

geothermal—involving heat produced deep inside the earth; geothermal power refers to the conversion of geothermal energy to electric power (56)

grounding—attachment of electrical equipment to a conductor embedded in the earth to allow excess current to drain safely into the ground (29)

insulator—a substance or object that conducts electric current poorly (26)

ion—an atom or molecule with an electric charge created because of a difference in the numbers of electrons and protons that it contains (27)

isogonic line—a line on a map that connects points with the same magnetic declination (46)

joule—a unit of energy (12)

magnetic declination—the angle between imaginary lines drawn from a point on the earth to the magnetic north pole and to the geographic or true north pole (46)

magnetic field—a region of space around a magnet in which the force of the magnet on another object depends on the position of that object (46)

magnetic north—the direction in which a compass points on the surface of the earth; the direction in which the magnetic north pole of the earth lies (46)

magnetometer—a device for measuring the strength of a magnetic field (47)

myelin—a layer of fatty material that insulates the neurons of vertebrates (75)

nerve—a bundle of neurons that carries information between the central nervous system and some other part of the body (75)

nerve impulse—an action potential (74)

neuron—a nerve cell (72)

neutron—a particle in the nucleus of an atom that is as heavy as a proton but has no electrical charge (5)

nucleus—the center of an atom; the nucleus consists of one or more protons and usually neutrons (5)

ohm—a unit of electrical resistance; one volt causes a current of one ampere to flow through an object with a resistance of one ohm (18)

Current Thoughts

Ohm's Law—the principle that voltage is equal to current multiplied by resistance: $V = IR$ (18)

oxidation—loss of electrons by an ion, atom, or molecule (35)

parallel circuit—a branched circuit in which current is divided among two or more parallel paths (17)

passive transport—movement of substances through a liquid, gas, or membrane by diffusion without the aid of energy provided by living cells (70)

peripheral nervous system—the part of the nervous system consisting of nerves that connect the central nervous system to other parts of the body (64)

potential—(see **voltage** below)

power—the rate at which energy is converted to another form or is used to do work; power is measured in watts (18)

proton—a positively charged particle that makes up part of every atom; one or more protons are found in the nucleus of every atom (5)

reduction—gain of electrons by an ion, atom, or molecule (35)

response—any behavior that occurs as a result of a stimulus (63)

resting potential—the voltage across the cell membrane of a neuron when it is not producing an action potential (73)

selectively permeable—permitting some substances to pass but not others; cells are surrounded by selectively permeable membranes (69)

series circuit—a circuit with all parts arranged in a single loop so that the current has only one possible pathway (17)

spinal cord—the thick bundle of nerves that extends from the brain of vertebrates down through their spinal columns; the spinal cord connects the brain to the nerves throughout the body (64)

static electricity—charges that accumulate on objects but do not circulate in the form of a current (5)

stimulus—any change or influence (for example, light, touch, heat, cold, or sound) that can cause a living thing to produce a response (63)

synapse—the small gap between the tip of an axon and the dendrite or other cell that it stimulates (74)

true north—the direction across the earth's surface in which the geographic north pole lies (46)

turbine—a fan or propellerlike wheel that is turned by the flow of air, water, or another fluid across its blades; turbines can be attached to generators to produce electric power (54)

volt—a unit of electric energy; a volt provides one joule per coulomb of charge (12)

voltage (potential)—potential energy of an electric charge as measured in volts (12)

watt—one joule of energy per second (18)

For Further Study . . .

BOOKS AND ARTICLES

Cook, J., and Thomas Alva Edison Foundation. 1988. *The Thomas Edison Book of Easy and Incredible Experiments.* Arlington, VA: National Science Teachers Association.

Evans, W. 1983. *Anatomy and Physiology.* 3d ed. Englewood Cliffs, NJ: Prentice-Hall.

Fischbach, G. 1992. Mind and brain. *Scientific American* 267: 48 ff.

Manning, A., and M. Dawkins. 1992. *An Introduction to Animal Behaviour.* 4th ed. Cambridge, England: Cambridge University Press.

Project Wild. 1987. *Aquatic Project Wild.* Boulder, CO: Western Regional Environmental Education Council, Inc.

Schafer, L. 1992. *Taking Charge: An Introduction to Electricity.* Arlington, VA: National Science Teachers Association.

Stevens, C. 1980. The neuron. *Scientific American* 242: 88–118.

INTERNET

Agency for Instructional Technology (AIT):

- World Wide Web—http://www.ait.net

- *Technos,* a journal for education and technology—technos@ait.net

- Sales and marketing—ait@ait.net

South-Western Science:

- World Wide Web— http://science.swep.com

- Science Discussion List—To join, send an e-mail message to majordomo@list.thomson.com and in the body of the message include the words *subscribe swep–science.*

AUDIO/VIDEO

Brain Power (videotape). This program contains four segments, each lasting 8–12 minutes. Titles and subject matter are "The Sense of Sight," how animals and insects use their eyes; "The Human Brain," how the brain functions and controls behavior; "Civilization's Progress," major landmarks in human progress; and "The Written Word," the evolution of humankind's ability to record knowledge and history. This tape is available from the Video Project: Media for a Safe & Sustainable World, 200 Estates Drive, Ben Lomond, CA 95005.

The Brain (videotape). A 15-minute program that examines the three parts of the brain, the nervous system, and the function of neurons, this tape is one of 10 in *Our Human Body,* part of AIT's Science Source series. For more information, contact the Agency for Instructional Technology, P.O. Box A, Bloomington, IN 47402-0120.

The Mysteries of Motion and Power (video tape). Each of the four segments in this program lasts 8–12 minutes. Titles and subject matter are "Considering Kinematics," understanding the science of motion; "Newton's Laws," the three laws that govern the motion of all bodies; "Electricity: A Current Affair," what electricity is and how it is produced; "The Physics of Force," the forces that create movement." The tape is available from the Video Project: Media for a Safe & Sustainable World, 200 Estates Drive, Ben Lomond, CA 95005.

What Is Electricity? (videotape). This is one of six 15-minute programs in *Physics: What*

Matters, What Moves, part of the Science Source series from AIT. It explores the role of matter and atoms in electrical charges. To order, contact the Agency for Instructional Technology, P.O. Box A, Bloomington, IN 47402-0120.

LEARNING TOOLS

Action Potential Experiments (software). Demonstrations and simulated experiments explore how action potentials are produced and studied. This resource is available from Academic Software Development Group, BioQuest Library, Computer Science Center, Building 224, University of Maryland, College Park, MD 20742.

Producing Energy (software). This product uses animation and graphics to explain and simulate the phases of power generation. It helps you to learn how energy is produced and how different types of power plants affect people and the environment. The first part includes a quick tour of a power plant and detailed information on each step in the process of producing energy. The second part allows you to apply this information to real life. Simulated situations allow users to control climate, hours of usage, population, and other variables. For more information, contact Visual Touch of America, Inc., 1405 17th Avenue, Suite 205, Longview, WA 98632.

AGENCIES AND ORGANIZATIONS

American Solar Energy Society. Sample copies of the magazine *Solar Today* are available from this national association, which is dedicated to promoting the use of solar energy. The book *Elementary and Secondary Science Projects in Renewable Energy and Energy Efficiency* can be purchased. For more information, write the society at 2400 Central Avenue, Suite G-1, Boulder, CO 80301.

American Wind Energy Association. A free fact sheet on wind energy is available from this organization, which advances the use of wind-energy technology. For more information, write the association at 122 C Street, N.W., Suite 400, Washington, DC 20001.

Energy Source Education Council. This nonprofit organization develops and distributes educational programs about energy. Its Energy Source Education Program receives financial support from utility companies. The programs are sold to member companies, which then distribute the materials free to schools in their service areas. For a free catalog, write the Program Distribution Office, 5505 E. Carson Street, Suite 250, Lakewood, CA 90713.

National Science Foundation. This federal agency supports basic science and engineering research and education. One of its many activities is to recruit scientific and technical personnel to advise young people about careers in science. For information, write the Office of Legislative and Public Affairs, 4201 Wilson Boulevard, Room 1245, Arlington, VA 22230.

U.S. Department of Energy. For a free copy of the department's catalog of educational programs, write the Office of Scientific and Technical Information, P.O. Box 62, Oak Ridge, TN 37831-9939.

ILLUSTRATIONS AND PHOTOS

Illustration Credits— Mike Cagle, 3, 5, 6, 11, 15, 16, 23, 27, 28, 34, 49, 51, 53, 62, 70, 71, 73, 74; Corel Corporation, 4, 17, 40; Brenda Grannan, icons; Jay Hagenow, 47; Heck's Pictorial Archive of Nature and Science, Dover Publications, 35; Vance Lawry, 64 (all)

Photo Credits—Corel Corporation, 5, 7, 20, 21, 22, 24, 26, 28, 29, 33, 36, 39, 42, 45, 46, 61, 62, 63, 72, 77; (Damasio, H., T. Grabowski, R. Frank, A.M. Galaburda, A.R. Damasio. 1994. The return of Phineas Gage: Clues about the brain from the skull of a famous patient. *Science* 264:1102–1105. Department of Neurology and Image Analysis Facility, University of Iowa), 65; NASA, 78; National Renewable Energy Laboratory (Warren Gretz, 54, 58; Sandia National Laboratories, 55); Photodisc, 56, 60; Public Service Indiana, 13, 19